CANADA
UNDER ATTACK

*Irish-American veterans of the Civil War and their
Fenian campaign to conquer Canada*

CHERYL MacDONALD

JAMES LORIMER & COMPANY LTD., PUBLISHERS
TORONTO

James Lorimer & Company Ltd., Publishers acknowledges the support of the Ontario Arts Council. We acknowledge the support of the Canada Council for the Arts which last year invested $24.3 million in writing and publishing throughout Canada. We acknowledge the Government of Ontario through the Ontario Media Development Corporation's Ontario Book Initiative.

Cover design: Meredith Bangay
Cover image: Library & Archives Canada, C-018737

Library and Archives Canada Cataloguing in Publication

MacDonald, Cheryl, 1952-, author
Canada under attack : Irish-American veterans of the
Civil War and their Fenian campaign to conquer Canada / Cheryl
MacDonald.

(Amazing stories collection)
Includes bibliographical references and index.
Issued in print and electronic formats.
ISBN 978-1-4594-0952-1 (paperback).--ISBN 978-1-4594-0953-8 (epub)

1. Canada--History--Fenian Invasions, 1866-1870. 2. Fenians.
3. Canada--Relations--United States. 4. United States--Relations--
Canada. I. Title. II. Series: Amazing stories (Toronto, Ont.)

FC480.F4M23 2015   971.04'8   C2015-903547-3
C2015-903548-1

James Lorimer & Company Ltd., Publishers
317 Adelaide Street West, Suite 1002
Toronto, ON, Canada
M5V 1P9
www.lorimer.ca

Printed and bound in Canada.

Dedicated with many thanks to
Dr. Stephen Kelly
and
Dr. Alvaro Figueredo,
of Hamilton's Juravinski Cancer Centre,
without whose skill and care
this book could not have been written.

Contents

Prologue

June 1, 1866, Black Rock (Buffalo), New York — *May was slipping into June as the men began loading into boats and barges under a moon just a few days past full. There were perhaps a thousand of them, some in green tunics, some in American Union Army uniforms with green facings, others in green shirts or civilian garb, as well as a handful in Confederate uniforms. Just a few days earlier they had hired two steam tugs and four barges, under the pretext of transporting hundreds of revellers to a company picnic at Falconwood, a resort on Grand Island.*

As the motley crew boarded their various transports, a small contingent moved more swiftly. Commanded by Colonel George Owen Starr, an American Civil War veteran who had fought with the Second Kentucky Cavalry, the advance party quickly captured a Buffalo tug, the J. H. Doyle, *along with a lumber barge owned by John and Thomas Conlon of Thorold, Ontario. Dressed in blue Union uniforms with green facings, and armed with Springfield .58 muzzle-loaders, the men moved relentlessly westward across the Niagara River to the Canadian side. At 1:30 a.m. they landed at Lower Ferry, a hamlet about a mile north of Fort Erie.*

After they streamed out of their vessels, their first order of business was to plant a flag. A large green banner, emblazoned with a gold Irish harp rather than the golden sunburst typical of Fenian flags, was unfurled. Then the men fanned out, subduing residents of the tiny settlement. Leaving a few behind to guard the captives, the rest of the party rushed towards Fort Erie to rendezvous with other invaders.

But they had not arrived undetected. A group of young men fishing by torchlight between Lower Ferry and Fort Erie had caught sight of the Doyle and barge as they plied the waters of the river. For days, rumours had been circulating that the Fenians would invade Canada. Now it was happening! The young men hurried to their wagons and horses, losing no time as they raced to raise the alarm.

Chapter 1
The Fenians

Europe was in upheaval. For years, a liberal movement had been growing. It advocated nationalism, equality, more political power for all men, and improved workers' rights. In early 1848, these ideas led to uprisings, most of which were relatively bloodless. It started in Sicily in January, followed by France in February, then southwest Germany, Hungary, and Denmark in March.

Members of Young Ireland watched with growing interest. Since English expansion into Ireland in 1169, and especially after Henry VIII declared himself King of Ireland in the 1530s, the Irish had seen the loss of their political power and systematic discrimination against their language and the Roman Catholic religion. The push for an independent Irish

Thomas D'Arcy McGee

state resulted in numerous revolts and uprisings, as well as legal reforms, but by the 1840s the majority of Irish were still second-class citizens in their own country. Although politicians, notably Daniel O'Connell, were making progress towards expanded Irish rights, events were moving far too slowly for many, including those who belonged to the Young Ireland movement.

After watching the events in Europe, the leaders of Young Ireland determined it was time for action. Ireland had fallen into hard economic times, made worse by *an Gorta Mór* (the Great Hunger). Beginning in 1845, when the country had a population of about 8.5 million, a disease had attacked the potatoes that were almost the sole source of food for about one in three Irish. Starvation, malnutrition, and disease would kill a million Irish between 1845 and 1852 and cause another million to leave the country.

Meanwhile, the British government did little to relieve the situation, fuelling the anger of nationalists, such as the Young Irelanders. The fury over the famine, plus the inspiration of the revolts on the European continent, they reasoned, might combine to win Irish independence once and for all. But the British government, realizing what had happened on the continent could spread to the United Kingdom, suspended the long-established right of British subjects to *habeas corpus* on July 22, 1848. This made it possible for the government to imprison without trial anyone accused of a crime.

It was too much for the Young Irelanders. On July 23,

the leaders called for open revolt, travelling through the counties of Wexford, Kilkenny, and Tipperary. On July 29, matters came to a head at the small village of The Commons, when supporters of Young Ireland leader William Smith O'Brien barricaded an area to prevent his arrest. When a group of Irish constabulary approached, the rebels chased them. The forty-seven policemen took shelter in a two-storey farmhouse, where they found the five children of widow Margaret McCormack and held them hostage.

In response to pleas from Mrs. McCormack, O'Brien persuaded the constabulary to free the children and shook hands with some of the officers through the window of the house. Then one of the policemen opened fire and a battle erupted. James Stephens and another Young Irelander dragged O'Brien to safety and were both wounded in the process.

The shooting went on for several hours. The constabulary in the McCormack house were running low on ammunition, but it became clear that reinforcements were on the way. The rebels dispersed. The leaders of Young Ireland became hunted men. Some, including O'Brien, were captured and transported to Bermuda or Van Diemen's Land (Australia). Others managed to escape. James Stephens, who had pulled O'Brien out of the line of fire, and another young man, John O'Mahony, made it safely to France, and O'Mahony eventually sailed for the United States. At the time the fighting erupted at The Commons, another Young

Irelander, twenty-two-year-old Thomas D'Arcy McGee, was in Scotland recruiting for the cause. At the age of seventeen, McGee had emigrated to the United States from Ireland with a sister. Over the next few years, he had a successful career as a writer, orator, and eloquent voice for Irish independence. Because of his work, in 1845 he was invited to return to Ireland and write for the *Freeman's Journal* in Dublin. This led to his involvement in the Young Ireland movement. McGee was back in Ireland by July 31, 1848. Although there was constant risk he would be recognized as an activist and arrested, he tried to rally his countrymen to finish what had been started at the McCormack farmhouse, frequently posing as a student studying for the priesthood as he travelled around. Unable to drum up support for an armed revolt, he left for America on September 1.

At this time, McGee was a married man with a young family. Although he resumed his career in the U.S. and continued to impress audiences and readers, he became disillusioned with American republicanism and the discrimination directed at Irish Catholics. By the spring of 1857 he had moved to Montreal, where he decided to enter politics.

In the interim, two of his cronies, James Stephens and John O'Mahony, were again working for Irish independence. Although exiled for a period, Stephens had returned to Ireland in 1856. On St. Patrick's Day 1857, discussions with Stephens resulted in the formation of a new organization, the Irish Revolutionary Brotherhood. Its purpose was to achieve independence for Ireland. The following year, in New York City, James Stephens was made "supreme organizer and director" of the Irish Revolutionary Brotherhood in America. Within a short time, Stephens renamed the organization the Fenians.

The name harked back to ancient Ireland and the Gaelic *fianna*, legendary warriors who roamed the land under the leadership of Finn MacCool. The nineteenth-century Fenians were organized into branches known as circles, with one man as its "centre." Under him were nine captains, each of whom had nine sergeants, under each of whom were nine privates. In theory, each circle contained about 730 members, although some could be larger.

One of the Fenians' main goals was to raise money from the Irish in North America, in order to support revolutionary activities back in Ireland. But there was also constant talk of taking more direct action in the New World. The Fenians believed that they could count on widespread support in both the United States and the British North American colonies: the United Province of Canada (which was made up of Canada East and Canada West, equivalent to modern Quebec and Ontario), Nova Scotia, New Brunswick, and Prince Edward Island. In New York and Boston, about one in every six people was Irish. In Montreal, one in four was either Irish-born or of Irish descent.

In Canada, many Irish had settled in the Maritimes, especially the so-called "famine" Irish. Economics was one reason for this settlement pattern. Conditions were so bad at home that those who emigrated could not afford the additional fare that might take them to Montreal or Canada West. In addition, before and during the famine a number of Irish landlords decided that, rather than shouldering the burden of caring for their poor and destitute tenants — which the law required — they would pay to send them to Canada by the cheapest means possible.

As a result, many of the Irish who came into Canada in the 1840s were starving, had little more than the clothes on their backs, and often were suffering from disease, which sometimes sparked epidemics once they arrived in Canada. Although many had some familiarity with the English language, others did not. Their clothing and customs were different. In addition, they were predominantly Roman Catholic, and the majority of English-speaking Canadians were not. Although the Irish had been immigrating to Canada for a very long time, the floodgates opened by the famine made them highly visible, and their many differences resulted in discrimination. They were often kept out of jobs, except the most menial, poorest paying, and most physically demanding ones.

This led to horrible living and working conditions and hopelessness, which in turn often led to alcoholism and violence. Some of the violence was within the Irish immigrant community, as they had brought old quarrels with them from the Old Country. Often, it was directed at others. One group with which Irish-Catholic immigrants frequently clashed were the Orangemen, members of the Orange Order. Named for William of Orange, who ruled Britain with his wife Mary from 1689 to 1702, the Orange Order at its best was a fraternal organization that supported good citizenship and loyalty to the British crown. But it was also staunchly Protestant, banning Catholics and certain Protestant denominations from membership and actively working to keep them on the fringes of society. The friction between Orangemen and Catholics was so great that by 1860 the Orange Order had been banned in Britain. Not so in Canada, but its reputation was such that when the Prince of Wales toured the country in 1860, his handlers refused to visit communities if the Orange Order was formally represented on the welcoming committees. Even so, the Orange Order was so widespread in Canada West and so influential that local authorities sometimes ignored those directions and Orange Order members turned out in full force.

Meanwhile, the Irish Catholics had their own societies, but these tended to be mutual benefit groups, where members contributed funds to help those who were sick or unemployed. The Fenians, on the other hand, had a very clear political agenda, which appealed to many, even if they did not join the organization. Those who disapproved of violence could still support the Fenians' goal of an independent Ireland. Fenian groups and supporters were part of the Irish-Canadian community. Their presence fed into the racism and hostility of the surrounding community towards the Irish. Irish immigrants were often portrayed as ignorant, violent, drunken, and incompetent. Typical was a report which appeared in the Toronto *Globe* in 1864. The most influential newspaper in the Canadian colonies, it was owned by George Brown, who was hostile towards the Irish. The *Globe* portrayed the Hibernian Benevolent Society as the same as the Fenians. Many believed that all Irish were Fenians and that all Fenians were terrorists just waiting for an opportunity to attack.

A majority of Irish Canadians worked hard and tried to improve their conditions of life, and were not supportive of the Fenians. The group was a secret society, and the church frowned on secret societies. Fenians were willing to use violence to achieve independence for Ireland. More moderate advocates of equality and rights for the Irish in Canadian society, including D'Arcy McGee, saw Fenians as a dangerous threat to political life and to acceptance of Irish Canadians in Canadian society.

Most Canadians were more worried about the physical threat posed by the Fenians, especially after the American Civil War. And the worry was not limited to Fenians: many American politicians in this period talked openly about annexation of Canada as the next logical step in the territorial expansion of the United States. The American government had already vastly extended its territory by taking over Florida, the Midwest territory that previously belonged to France, California, and Texas. When the American Civil War began in April 1861, the Fenians were just starting to get organized. Many of their leaders welcomed the war as a golden opportunity for training. The experience of military discipline and skill in using firearms would be very useful in the battle to free Ireland. In addition, the war was also seen as a means of diverting British attention from Ireland.

Britain was officially neutral in the Civil War, and this meant Canada (still a British colony) was as well. Still, there were incidents. A Union naval captain, Charles Wilkes, stopped a British mail packet, RMS *Trent*, in November 1861 and took as captives two Confederate envoys on their way to Britain and France. Wilkes's action sparked an international incident and talk of British involvement in the Civil War, at least until the two Confederates were released several weeks later. As the war progressed, Britain took advantage of a legal loophole, despite official neutrality, and allowed Confederate warships to be built and launched in British shipyards. They did considerable damage to Union ships and the American government insisted that Britain was partly responsible. Meanwhile, Canada was used as a base by Confederate spies and agitators, including a group that staged a series of robberies in St. Albans, Vermont, in October 1864. The group killed at least one man, but their charges were dismissed on a technicality by a Montreal magistrate. In Nova Scotia, Confederate representatives operated relatively openly, and Nova Scotia merchants grew rich on selling much-needed supplies to the Confederacy.

The Fenians

In the aftermath of the Vermont raid, United States newspapers called for an attack on Canada and cancellation of the Rush-Bagot treaty, which had minimized armed ships on the Great Lakes after the War of 1812. Neither happened, but in late 1864 relations between Britain and Canada on the one side and the Unionist United States government on the other were so strained that a number of militia units were called up ready to defend the borders.

A few months later, in May 1865, the American Civil War finally came to an end with the defeat of the Confederacy. Within a very short time, thousands of battle-hardened soldiers found themselves with little to do. Diplomatic relations between the United States and Britain were still strained. In addition, a large number of Americans believed in "manifest destiny" — the idea that they were fated to occupy the entire North American continent, including the British Canadian colonies. With the war over, the time seemed ripe for the American population to expand westward — and possibly northward. At one point, in negotiations between Britain and the United States, American negotiators proposed that, in compensation for damages done by the *Alabama* and other British-built Confederate warships, Britain should turn over parts of British Columbia, the Red River Colony (around Winnipeg, in what would later become the province of Manitoba), and the province of Nova Scotia.

That did not happen, but, as the Fenians looked northward, American authorities tended to look the other way.

The Irish vote was too important for American politicians to ignore and, since the Americans were already ticked off with the British, allowing the Fenians to make threatening gestures had its advantages. At one point, the British ambassador in Washington, Sir Frederick Bruce, complained to American Secretary of State William H. Seward about the Fenian activities, which not only were hostile, but also broke neutrality laws. Seward's response was that the Fenians' activity was grossly exaggerated and that "nothing would serve as much to give it importance as that it become the subject of official correspondence." In other words, Seward was suggesting, ignore them and they'll go away.

Canadian authorities took the Fenians far more seriously. Future prime minister John A. Macdonald commented to Governor General Lord Monck that the Fenian movement "must not be despised, either in America or Ireland. I am so strongly of that opinion that I shall spare no expense in watching them on both sides of the line." D'Arcy McGee was far less diplomatic, referring to Fenianism as "a foreign disease" and "political leprosy." He was especially afraid that any hostile activities directed against the Canadian provinces by the Fenians would result in a huge and potentially deadly backlash against Irish Canadians, and that it almost certainly would be led by members of the Orange Order.

Until the fall of 1865, there was little evidence of a Fenian plan to invade Canada. That changed at a conference in Philadelphia when a small but vocal group led by William

The Fenians

Randall Roberts, a dry goods merchant, and Thomas Sweeny, a former brigadier general in the Union Army, began to encourage an attack on Canada. No motion was passed at the meeting. The official Fenian policy in North America stayed the same — send money and weapons back to Ireland. But the idea of an attack on British North America started to gain ground, especially after a split in the Fenian ranks. In January 1866, followers of John O'Mahony held another convention in New York, at which they made it clear they were opposed to an invasion of Canada. The next month, Roberts's supporters gathered in Pittsburgh, where they voted in favour of Sweeny's plan to proceed with an attack. Not long after, word of the decision filtered back to Canadian authorities, who braced themselves for an invasion they suspected would take place on St. Patrick's Day — March 17, 1866.

Chapter 2
Spies and Secret Police

Although the Fenians were a secret society, a good deal of information about them circulated, especially in newspapers aimed at the Irish community such as Toronto's *Irish Canadian* and New York's *Irish American*. The information was not necessarily reliable, though, and there were always certain details that were supposed to be kept secret. To defend against any possible invasion, separating truth from rumours and uncovering clandestine plans became the mission of Canadian authorities.

A key line of defence was the Western Frontier Constabulary, forerunner of the Dominion Police Service, which eventually evolved into the Royal Canadian Mounted Police. At its head was Gilbert McMicken, a Scot who had immigrated to Canada as a young man and settled in the Niagara area. Starting in the freight forwarding business, he expanded into other commercial enterprises and into politics, helped in part by his wife's family connections. Ann Theresa Duff was the granddaughter of Alexander Grant, a key player in Upper Canada's fur trade who had served for a brief time as lieutenant governor of the province. Grant was also related by marriage to the family of Robert Hamilton, a prominent and wealthy Scot. By the time he was twenty-five, McMicken had been appointed collector of customs at Queenston.

His varied business interests led to his foray into politics, which, among other things, saw him elected first mayor of Clifton (now Niagara Falls) and later MLA for Welland. In his political career, McMicken grew close to future prime minister John A. Macdonald. It appears McMicken may have given Macdonald some financial help and his support was definitely appreciated. Macdonald described McMicken as "a shrewd, cool and determined man" who could be relied on to carry out whatever duties were assigned him. McMicken had moved to Essex County, at the westernmost end of the province, in 1860 and served as a magistrate. In November 1864 Macdonald was instrumental in having him appointed excise officer in Windsor. A more important appointment soon followed.

Gilbert McMicken

The St. Albans raid had recently taken place and Canada East and Canada West were on high alert. Realizing that more had to be done to protect both parts of the united province, the government created the country's first secret service. McMicken was appointed stipendiary magistrate for Canada West, as well as justice of the peace, while Frederick William Ermatinger was given similar posts in Canada East. Born in Sault Ste-Marie in 1811, Ermatinger had ties through marriage and family connections to both the British military in Montreal and French-Canadian society, which helped advance his career. At one time police commissioner, and then police superintendent, for Montreal, in 1855 he became field inspector for the active volunteer militia in Canada East. Ermatinger's years of experience proved useful when the new secret service was formed. Both he and McMicken understood conditions on the border between Canada and the U.S. and took the time to cultivate contacts with Americans in border towns so they could be informed of any trouble that was brewing.

Initially, the focus was on making sure there was no repeat of the St. Albans raid or any other violation of neutrality laws. In McMicken's case, a great deal of time was spent watching out for illegal military drills or the activities of "substitute brokers" — those who offered Canadians money to take the place of Americans in the Union Army. McMicken's force, which was for a time referred to as the Western Frontier Constabulary, never numbered more than two dozen. Most of them were large young men with a background in policing or military service. They were deployed in key towns along railroad lines and along the border. McMicken's agents were stationed in Amherstburg, Berlin (now Kitchener), Cobourg, Dunnville, Guelph, Hamilton, London, Paris, Port Colborne, Port Dalhousie, Port Maitland, Port Robertson, Port Stanley, St. Catharines, St. Thomas, Stratford, and Toronto. They received about $30 a month, a respectable salary for the era, although payment was not always timely. In addition, the agents were often out of pocket because they initially paid for their own expenses, and most of them travelled frequently, moving quickly from one town to another. (When they did not travel,

McMicken urged them to get jobs. This would allow them to blend more easily into the community than they would by merely hanging around ports, railway stations, or hotels.)

The agents were not always welcomed by local authorities, some of whom described them as incompetent, stupid, slow, or drunk. But they did get some support, not only in Canada, but also in some U.S. border towns, such as Detroit and Buffalo, where American officials allowed them to gather information without interference.

The results were initially disappointing, since the agents who were hired weren't necessarily well trained or suited for the job. A number of them were fired soon after they were hired. Making matters more complicated, they routinely paid for information, which likely encouraged informants to exaggerate or fabricate reports. But, gradually, McMicken built a force of reliable men. After the Civil War ended, their focus shifted to the Fenian problem. Some of them were ordered to pose as Fenians and join circles in Chicago, Cincinnati, Detroit, and other locations.

McMicken also thought it would be useful to have female agents, to entice Fenians to give up their secrets. "One or two Clever Women whose absolute virtue stands questioned by the Censorious," was how he described them to John A. Macdonald. It is not clear whether he ever actually had such female agents, but it does show the lengths to which McMicken was willing to go to discover what the Fenians were up to.

Even so, the information gathered was not always reliable. At one point, based on what the secret service was able to uncover, Sir John Michel, who commanded British forces in Canada, declared that in Canada East the Fenian movement could "hardly be said to exist" and that there were only "limited" traces in Canada West. In fact, there was considerable evidence of Fenian activity. In January 1865, one agent reported to McMicken that there was a Fenian circle just outside London, while another claimed there were three in Guelph. By May, there was a report of a lodge in Clifton, near Niagara Falls. By the end of the year, one agent claimed there were at least seventeen lodges in Canada West, with nine of them in Toronto.

In September, an agent, Patrick Nolan, had been stationed in Chicago. From there he advised that the Fenians had amassed a large quantity of arms and were planning to buy gunboats. Nolan urged McMicken to ask the government to call out the militia. Later in the year, agents reported from Sarnia that a Fenian invasion was expected as soon as the St. Clair River froze, and that in preparation weapons and ammunition had been shipped to Canada in six coffins.

McMicken took his agents' reports with many grains of salt. As far as he was concerned, a great deal of deliberate exaggeration originated from the Fenians themselves, who wanted to convince the public that they not only had the support of the American government, but also had more than enough weapons to carry out their plans. As a result, the decisions made regarding the defence of Canada against a possible Fenian raid were based partly on intelligence, partly on the gut feelings of McMicken and his colleagues.

In addition to McMicken's and Ermatinger's men, others provided information to the government. British consuls in American cities shared reports of Fenian activities. Among them was Edward Archibald, who was based in New York, but had been born in Nova Scotia.

Meanwhile, supporters of D'Arcy McGee did what they could to infiltrate the Fenians, or at least pass along whatever information they could glean. And McMicken himself was not adverse to going into the field. In October 1865, while the Fenian Senate was meeting at the Astor House hotel in New York, McMicken was among the hotel guests.

By this time, fears of Fenian activity were growing. Back in September 1865, James Stephens had led a rising in Ireland. When it failed, the Fenians shifted the focus of their activities to North America. Watching the events unfold, John A. Macdonald authorized McMicken to hire another five or six men. "The Fenian action in Ireland is serious," Macdonald warned. "We must not be caught napping."

The following month, rumours of a pending invasion reached such a peak that ten thousand militiamen were called out to patrol the borders. McMicken thought the invasion would take place on November 5. No invasion materialized, but by early 1866 McMicken had learned that Fenian sympathizers were stockpiling weapons in a Toronto residence and that there was talk of bringing other arms into Fort Erie from Buffalo. Piecing bits of information together, it seemed that the Fenians were planning an attack of some sort in Canada West on St. Patrick's Day — March 17, 1866. A week before the feast day of Ireland's patron saint, McMicken telegraphed Macdonald to tell him that five thousand Fenians were heading for Detroit.

Meanwhile, McMicken tried to minimize the problem of Fenian sympathizers in Canada by visiting Toronto and meeting with Michael Murphy, a tavern keeper and cooper who was also the founder and first president of the Hibernian Benevolent Society of Canada. Although he had repeatedly and publicly denied it, Murphy was a Fenian. The Hibernian Society was supposed to help the community and provided defence against anti-Irish factions, notably the Orange Order, which prompted them to conduct military drills. Observers assumed they were preparing for a Fenian invasion, further inflaming anti-Irish feeling. With Canadians on alert, convinced that a Fenian attack was pending, it seemed foolhardy to stage a St. Patrick's Day parade in Toronto. The St. Patrick's Society sensibly agreed to cancel any demonstrations on that date, but Murphy and his Hibernians were adamant. The most he would do was promise McMicken that it would be a peaceful demonstration. To further ensure that violence was kept to a minimum, McMicken also persuaded Toronto's mayor, F. H. Medcalf, to allow the parade to take place without any official interference. Medcalf agreed, but two thousand soldiers were standing by, ready to intervene if the six hundred Hibernians who marched in the parade caused any trouble.

Fortunately, nothing significant occurred. This, as well as the false alarm in November, persuaded McMicken that the reports of an impending Fenian invasion were off-target, and that there was no serious threat to worry about. He couldn't have been more wrong.

* * *

While Canadian agents were gathering information about Fenian activities, a young Englishman was doing his part to undermine the organization. Henri Le Caron had served in the Union Army, rising to the rank of major before his discharge in February 1866. Although he had passed himself off as French, he was, in fact, an Englishman named Thomas Billis Beach. Born in Colchester, England, he was an adventurous and troublesome boy who repeatedly ran away from home and refused to settle into the apprenticeship his father had arranged for him. He eventually ended up in Paris, where he made the acquaintance of a number of Americans. When the Civil War began, he and some of his friends decided to enlist. Knowing he would be breaking British law by enlisting, Thomas changed his name when he joined the Eighth Pennsylvanian Reserves.

He planned to serve for three months, but instead stayed

for the duration of the war, surviving battles and other dangers, including capture by Confederate marauders. Although small and wiry, Le Caron was brave, had a good presence, and was usually able to win people's confidence. After the war, he married a Tennessee girl and settled in Nashville, where he began studying medicine.

At some point he had started writing letters to his father back in England, filling them with details of his life, some having to do with his friendship with another former Union officer, John O'Neill, who was becoming prominent in the Fenian movement. Le Caron's father, John, well aware of the trouble the Fenians were causing in Ireland, showed his son's letters to the local member of Parliament, who forwarded the information to the Home Office.

Soon afterwards, John Beach wrote his son asking him to provide as much information as possible about O'Neill and his Fenian colleagues. The information would be passed along to the Home Office and might prove useful in thwarting Fenian plans. As time went along, Le Caron was also urged to join the Fenian ranks and make himself as useful as possible to O'Neill.

Although Le Caron was not one of McMicken's agents, McMicken and a select few in the government were aware of his activities. Eventually, Le Caron's undercover assignment would lead him to an invasion of Canada.

Chapter 3
Taking Aim at New Brunswick

New Brunswick was a booming province in 1865. Its strong economy was based mainly on timber and shipbuilding. Its population of about 270,000 was flourishing and generally peaceful. Saint John, the largest town, was home to about 42,000, making it comparable in size to Toronto or Quebec City. The anti-Irish violence that had followed after the province was used as a dumping ground for Irish immigrants fleeing famine conditions had largely faded. Now New Brunswickers were mainly concerned with progress, both economic and political.

One major issue of the day was Confederation.

Although some, including New Brunswick's Lieutenant Governor Arthur Hamilton Gordon, favoured a union of New Brunswick, Nova Scotia, and Prince Edward Island, Canadian politicians and the British government were pushing for a confederation among Maritimes, Canada East, and Canada West. In the summer of 1864, D'Arcy McGee led a delegation of about one hundred people from the Canadas on a tour of New Brunswick. Amid the receptions, speeches, and tours, friendly relations were forged that would ultimately be solidified in 1867.

In the meantime, there was some friction with the American neighbours in Maine. Half a century earlier, during the War of 1812, the residents of New Brunswick and Maine had largely ignored the hostilities between their two governments and continued trading and socializing. The American Civil War had been somewhat different. A certain number of New Brunswickers had sided with the Confederacy, and some Confederates had used the province as a base.

The *Chesapeake* affair was one notorious example. On December 7, 1863, while travelling from Portland, Maine, to New York City, the steamer *Chesapeake* was seized by several passengers, who turned out to be Confederate sympathizers. Among them were some Maritimers. After restraining the crew, the captors headed for Saint John, refueled and moved on to Halifax, but ran out of coal near the mouth of the harbour. Although some locals provided assistance to the hijackers, she was captured by a U.S. cruiser on December 12. An international controversy erupted, with Confederates claiming that she was a prize of war and the U.S. had acted illegally by taking her in British waters. The furor soon petered out, but it was viewed as evidence of Maritimers' hostility towards the Northern states.

Further evidence of this hostility arose in 1864 when a band of Confederate soldiers led by Captain William Collins gathered in St. Stephen, crossed the St. Croix River, and tried to rob the bank in Calais, Maine. They were arrested and imprisoned, but when Collins escaped he returned to New Brunswick to hide from American authorities.

After the war ended, the bitter feeling on both sides of the border lingered. Adding to this were fears that Americans would turn their attention northward. Should that happen, New Brunswickers were prepared. This had not always been the case. In 1852, the legislative assembly had stopped spending money for defence, convinced that there was little chance of an American attack. Besides, the British navy and army could be counted on to repel any invaders. Then responsible government was introduced, and, in Britain, a movement to reduce or eliminate the cost of defending the provinces began. Soon after Gordon became lieutenant governor in 1861, he set about building a militia that could be counted on in case of emergency.

Just such an emergency seemed to be approaching in the fall of 1865. In September, acting on information provided by spies, the British government closed *The Irish*

People, a Fenian newspaper published in Ireland, arrested staff members and other sympathizers, and the Fenian organization in Ireland crumbled. It now fell to the North American section of the movement to take action that would lead to Irish liberation. At the convention in Philadelphia in October, the faction led by William Randall Roberts called for invading British North America, while John O'Mahony's faction preferred to focus on raising funds and gathering arms for Ireland. A Fenian Senate was created, led by Roberts, and O'Mahony lost much of his power.

For the time being there were no official plans to invade Canada, but the Fenians' increasingly vocal militancy raised Canadians' fears. In early November 1865, at the same time as Canada West and Canada East were calling up militia to guard the borders against a possible attack, Lieutenant Governor Gordon heard from British Colonial Secretary Edward Cardwell that there was a possibility that Fenians would use Maine as a base from which to attack New Brunswick. Other reports followed, including a warning from D'Arcy McGee, repeated by Sir John Michel, commander of British troops in Canada, that Saint John should be watched carefully. While Gordon did not think there would be a full-scale invasion, he did anticipate a series of small raids, most likely on border towns. He also realized that it would be tricky to defend the thousand-kilometre border with Maine, since most militia members were located in larger towns, not in the smaller communities along the frontier. In addition, most militia members were employed, and if they were called up for border duty it would mean a cut in pay and possible loss of their jobs. As a result, Gordon developed a plan for border defence, but did not put it into action until he received a coded message from the British ambassador in Washington, Sir Frederick Bruce. According to Bruce's intelligence, a large Fenian attack was imminent.

To put his plan into action, Gordon needed to get the support of the citizens of various communities. On December 5, he headed for the frontier, having sent a message to provincial government leader Albert James Smith to join him in St. Stephen, close to the American border. Smith was seen travelling hurriedly through Saint John after dark in bad weather, prompting rumours that an invasion was imminent. The people of Saint John panicked. There was a run on the banks, the garrison of the town was put on high alert, and its commander telegraphed to Halifax requesting that a British warship be sent to the local harbour. Soon the rumours of a Fenian attack were telegraphed to other communities, including Fredericton and Woodstock, spreading the panic over a large part of the province.

As the citizenry braced for an invasion, Gordon called a meeting of St. Stephen's prominent citizens and proposed an alternative to calling up the militia. Although New Brunswick's militia numbered about 2,100 volunteers at the time, assembling them along the border would take time and money. So Gordon suggested the formation of a home guard, a group of local, brave, and able-bodied young men, whom he promised to arm with rifles. Since they were already on the spot, they would provide the first line of defence.

The plan was accepted enthusiastically and Gordon moved on to St. Andrews and Woodstock with the same proposal. In Woodstock, he stressed a slightly different theme, discussing his fears that the Fenian threat would widen the gap between Catholics and Protestants, creating bitterness that might never disappear. It was fundamentally the same message that D'Arcy McGee had delivered repeatedly in his speeches criticizing both the Fenians and the Orange Order.

An 1865 raid never materialized, but the fear of one resulted in the creation of a home guard in communities all along the New Brunswick–Maine border. The new year brought more threats, as both Gordon's informants and McMicken's spy network collected intelligence that suggested an attack would come on St. Patrick's Day, or possibly earlier. In New Brunswick, this led to fears that the home guard was inadequately armed, which in turn led to another run on the banks in Saint John.

By this time, the Fenians had split in two. In early January, a meeting organized in New York City was dominated by O'Mahony's supporters, who overturned the resolutions of the Philadelphia convention and once more emphasized their main agenda: raising support for Ireland. In response, Roberts's supporters held their own convention in Pittsburgh in February, at which Thomas "Fighting Tom"

Sweeny's strategy for an invasion was adopted. Sweeny had been a Union general. Just forty-five years old, the native of County Cork, Ireland, had enjoyed a distinguished military career, serving, among other places, at the Battle of Shiloh and during the Atlanta campaign. Like many American officers before him, he was convinced the conquest of British North America would be relatively easy.

Sweeny's experience and the plan he unveiled went a long way towards persuading the Roberts faction to stage an attack. But so did events in Britain, where Parliament had suspended *habeas corpus* in an attempt to keep civil unrest to a minimum. Authorities there had also arrested large numbers of Irish activists, including 150 Irish Americans.

Sweeny's plan called for a large army to attack Canada. As the promise of action convinced many Fenians to support Roberts's faction, O'Mahony's lieutenant, Bernard Doran Killian, watched in dismay. Killian was a journalist who had worked alongside D'Arcy McGee while McGee was living in the U.S. Frequently, when McGee was away on speaking engagements, Killian had filled in for him at the newspaper until McGee's more moderate approach to the Irish question had ended their friendship.

Recognizing that now was the time for action, Killian badgered O'Mahony to attack Canada, too. Killian had been part of a delegation that visited Washington, DC, to see President Andrew Johnson and Secretary of State William H. Seward. Both men were known to be sympathetic to the Irish

— although that may have been partly to curry the Irish vote. According to Killian, when Johnson and Seward were asked what they might do if the Fenians invaded British territory, the answer was rather vague, but encouraging: they would recognize "accomplished facts." While the politicians may have been obfuscating in order to preserve the Irish vote, Killian and his colleagues chose to interpret their answer to mean the United States would not interfere with a Fenian invasion. And, in view of how U.S. authorities had handled other situations — where Americans had moved into foreign territory and taken the law into their own hands, ultimately prompting annexation — they had good reason to think that the American government might support their initiative. In 1836, after years of friction, predominantly American settlers in the Mexican state of Texas had declared their independence. By the end of 1845, Texas had become the twenty-eighth American state.

On March 17, 1866, the day authorities in British North America were expecting an invasion, Killian proposed an attack on Campobello Island. There is some evidence that Killian believed the island was the centre of a territorial dispute between the U.S. and Britain. By capturing it, the Fenians would take it out of British hands, satisfying American expansionists and winning more supporters. There was also some hope that the international community would recognize it as Irish territory. With a Fenian government given legal status, the brotherhood could use Campobello as a base from which to attack British territory, including

Ireland. They might also issue letters of marque, documents that would allow shipowners to act as legal pirates and attack British ships on behalf of the Fenian government. Finally, the successful capture of Campobello Island would likely inspire the Irish of New Brunswick, who could then be counted on to support the Fenian cause.

The proposal was accepted and Killian got to work gathering money, weapons, and transportation. As usual, the plans were hardly a secret. Although the information that appeared in the press or reached the ears of the public in other ways was wildly exaggerated, there was enough truth to justify considerable anxiety.

According to one rumour, published in the *New York Herald* in early April 1866, three steamers, carrying three thousand veteran soldiers, had set out to attack Bermuda. Another report said an additional twenty-five hundred men had also set out on some other expedition of conquest.

Neither rumour was true, but there was still serious cause for alarm in the British colonies. During the December 1865 alert, Lieutenant Governor Gordon had asked British naval authorities in Halifax to send a gunboat to defend Saint John harbour, but nothing had been done. He repeated his request on February 1, 1866. This time, the response was to send HMS *Pylades*, a 1,278-ton steam corvette with a crew of 274. Although there was some discussion whether she should be deployed near Saint John or in Passamaquoddy Bay, she stayed in the Saint John area until April.

When St. Patrick's Day passed without an attack, Gordon and the military leadership took a close look at New Brunswick's defences. The most vulnerable locations were the widely scattered border towns. Conventional military wisdom held that, with such a large area to defend, forces should be held back until a threat materialized, and then sent where they were needed. This was the plan Major General Sir Charles Hastings Doyle favoured. Doyle was a veteran of the Crimean War who had command of the British forces in the lower provinces, and initially saw no reason to deviate from traditional practice. But Gordon saw the situation differently. Among other things, he worried that the communities who had willingly volunteered to create a home guard at the end of 1865 would feel abandoned if nothing was done to protect them. Doyle gave in to Gordon's wishes.

Slowly, in groups of six, ten, or twenty, Fenians drifted towards Maine's border with New Brunswick. Most them were armed, carrying pistols or knives but not much more. An obvious Fenian army would have been a clear violation of American neutrality laws, and so the men were sent to various border towns with not much more than they might carry while travelling on business. Meanwhile, rifles, cannon, and ammunition were gathered; a schooner, *Ocean Spray*, was leased; and preparations were made to send the arms separately.

On April 10, 1866, Robert Ker, the British vice-consul in Eastport, Maine, reported that one hundred Fenians had

York County Militia

arrived in the town. They were unarmed, their weapons having been held up by American authorities in Portland.

That same day saw two other developments. Killian reached Eastport with three colleagues. He rented a hall, which would serve both as his operational headquarters and as a gathering place for Fenians and the general public when Killian staged a speaking event. Other Fenians were in the town by this point, and they assisted in taking care of some of the arrangements. According to reports, a quantity of gunpowder was purchased for the creation of cartridges, and a local iron foundry had been requested to forge some cannon. Meanwhile, more Fenians trickled into town via boats, stagecoach, on horseback, or on foot. They staged drills at Eastport, across from St. Stephen, and Robbinston, across from St. Andrews, without any interference from American authorities. Meanwhile, Lieutenant Governor Gordon asked General Doyle to send one or two companies to the frontier. Doyle dilly-dallied, partly because he was worried about the possibility of desertion. This was an ongoing problem with the British army and navy when stationed close to the American border. It was far too easy to slip across to the United States, where financial opportunities were believed to be better. Complicating matters was the fact that the military had a significant Irish component. For generations, the relative lack of opportunities in Ireland had persuaded many to find employment in Her Majesty's service.

No one was sure just how many Fenians had converged on the American side of the St. Croix River. They tended to stay in small groups, in hopes of lessening official attention. Probably the number totalled a thousand at most, but that number fluctuated considerably as new men arrived and others departed.

Although American officials were slow to take action, the presence of so many strangers did cause concern. Rifles and cannon were not much in evidence, but that so many of these new arrivals had pistols or knives created some alarm for the safety of the residents even on the U.S. side of the border. In addition, there was still the issue of neutrality laws. Around mid-April, orders were given to send a U.S. navy squadron to Eastport. Five vessels were involved: USS *De Soto*, *Winooski*, *Augusta*, *Mantonomak*, and *Don*, with a combined total of thirty-six guns. They were to stay on the scene until any threat of a Fenian invasion passed. In addition, General George Gordon Meade, who had decisively defeated Robert E. Lee at Gettysburg, was sent to Eastport to deal with the Fenians.

Despite U.S. military and naval efforts, the Fenians went ahead with their plans. On the night of Friday, April 13, Dennis Doyle, the leader of the Calais Fenian circle, led two boats full of men across the St. Croix, landing just below St. Stephen. They were spotted by a local chap known as "Old Joe" Young, who raised the alarm, riding hellbent through the vicinity, pounding on doors and shouting, "Arm yourselves! The Fenians are upon you!" No full-scale attack materialized, however. After shooting off their guns and burning a few woodpiles, Doyle's band returned to the American side. But their presence and Young's warning terrified a number of New Brunswickers, some of whom abandoned their homes.

Another invasion followed on Saturday, April 14, when a group of men landed on Indian Island. The small dot of land in Passmaquoddy Bay had a little settlement, including some warehouses and a customs house. The main attraction for the Fenians seems to have been the customs house, over which a Union Jack flew. Shortly after midnight, customs officer James Dixon was wakened by pounding on the door and the sound of shutters being ripped off his window. Dixon found himself face to face with a band of armed intruders who demanded he take down the flag and give it to them. At first, he hesitated, but with the intruders threatening him with bodily harm and his wife panicking about the safety of their children, he gave in. The capture of the flag would be widely promoted for its propaganda value.

Elsewhere, there were other troubling signs of Fenian activity, including what seemed to be a Fenian steamer reconnoitering Partridge Island. At this point, Gordon again telegraphed Doyle. This time Doyle agreed to send troops.

On Monday, April 16, Killian held a rally in Calais. The gathering was reputedly attended by at least a thousand people, including some ladies from St. Stephen. In addition to Killian, one of the speakers was a Fenian who had lived in New Brunswick, Patrick A. Sinnott. During the course of their orations the men denied any plans to invade the province, but did call on the American government to support the Fenian cause in gratitude for the Irish-American lives lost during the Civil War. Claiming that Confederation was being forced upon its North American provinces by Britain, Killian and his crew also promised to protect New

Brunswick against that threat, and to remain close to the border until it had dissipated.

The very next day, April 17, the *Ocean Spray*, the steamer the Fenians had leased, arrived in Eastport with 129 cases of weapons destined for Colonel James Kerrigan, one of Killian's subordinates. The American collector of customs delayed delivery while he consulted the district attorney in Portland. The DA's ruling was that there was nothing he could do unless he could prove they were ultimately going to Canada or some other foreign jurisdiction. The *Ocean Spray* was released, but then was seized by USS *Winooski*, which had just arrived in harbour. A flurry of telegrams followed involving a number of interested parties, including U.S. government and military officials and British vice-consul Ker. On April 18, with matters still up in the air, General Meade reached Eastport and gave orders to remove the weapons and put them in Fort Sullivan. At least seven cases went missing while officials dithered. Ultimately, Ker reported that "more than 600 stands of arms, 197,000 rounds of ammunition, and a number of coehorns (short cannon or mortars) was among the cargo seized" and that, apparently, did not include the seven missing cases.

If a full-scale Fenian invasion had been planned for late April, the seizure of the cargo had thrown a wrench into those plans. The Fenians lingered, continuing to cause trouble, most of which was little more than mischief. From time to time, Fenians would walk across the bridge to St. Stephen, or militiamen would walk to the American side, with resulting harsh words and some physical violence, but nothing serious. And once again, Dennis Doyle, head of the Calais Fenians, ordered woodpiles set on fire, this time for four miles along the coast between Calais and Milltown. There is no record of "Old Joe" Young or anyone else riding about the countryside raising the alarm, but once more the people on the New Brunswick side of the river became convinced that an invasion was imminent and fled from their homes in terror.

On April 21, another party of Fenians attacked Indian Island. This time, they burned the warehouses and their contents — all of which belonged to Americans. Not much could be done about the incident, although Captain A. W. A. Hood of the *Pylades* was disciplined because it was felt that he should have been more vigilant in guarding the island against further Fenian incursions. On April 22, it was decided to put a military post on the island.

The most serious incident took place on April 28, when about fifty Fenians sailed aboard an aging schooner, *Two Friends*, which had been leased and was commanded by a Captain Colson. Spotting the cases of rifles, Colson refused to sail for Campobello Island until he was forced to do so at gunpoint. Near Lubec, the wind died and the customs inspector was able to board *Two Friends*. Seeing armed men aboard, he quickly retreated and alerted the authorities. Two American gunboats were assigned to chase down the schooner, but before they could get up enough steam, *Two*

Friends rounded a point of land and disappeared from view. By the time the gunboats were able to pursue her, she had vanished completely. In fact, during the time she was out of sight, *Two Friends* had come across another schooner, *Wentworth*, and had transferred all passengers and cargo to her. When the gunboats arrived the men, now on *Wentworth*, shouted that *Two Friends* had just rounded another and more distant point of land. The gunboats, still hoping to catch *Two Friends*, dashed off that way in pursuit. In fact, *Two Friends* by now was underwater, having been scuttled after the transfers. The Fenians returned to Eastport and cached their weapons, which were later found by a local resident.

The seizure of the *Ocean Spray* weapons, by pure chance, had apparently stopped any possibility of a successful Fenian invasion. By early May, the men who had been lingering along the Maine–New Brunswick border began to slowly disperse. There were still signs of organized activity, including a gathering at Doyle's house and a brief encounter between a sentry at Indian Island and a Fenian boat, which resulted in an exchange of gunfire. The Fenian vessel disappeared before any information could be ascertained about its mission.

The armaments taken off *Two Friends* were not enough to make up for the loss of weapons seized from *Ocean Spray.* Although there were occasional alarms through May, it eventually became clear that the Fenian threat was abating. Gradually, life returned to normal along the border. By

June 21, 1866, the last volunteers defending New Brunswick were able to return to civilian life.

The failed invasion had serious repercussions for the Fenians, or at least for the O'Mahony faction. There was much criticism and finger-pointing, eventually forcing O'Mahony's resignation and leaving the Roberts faction to carry on without them. The Fenians turned their attention westward.

Chapter 4
The Invasion of Canada West

In the late spring of 1866, rumours of another possible Fenian invasion were rampant. Experience had made the authorities extra cautious about false alarms, but by late May there were strong indications that something was going on. A large number of Irishmen and suspected Fenians were gathering in Buffalo, New York, just across the border from Canada West's Niagara Peninsula. On the afternoon of May 31, Colonel Patrick L. MacDougall, a British officer and commander of the Canadian militia, gave the order to send troops to Fort Erie.

Military authorities had hesitated almost to the last

possible moment. As MacDougall's orders were relayed to the militia in Toronto, Hamilton, and elsewhere, the Fenians were already launching their invasion. A couple of days earlier, some Fenians had rented two steamboats and four barges, claiming they were needed to transport a large group of people from a Buffalo company to a picnic on Grand Island, in the middle of the Niagara River. Before they were put into use, however, Lieutenant-Colonel George Owen Starr led his Seventeenth Kentucky Fenian Regiment in hijacking a steamer, the *J. H. Doyle*, as well as a Canadian lumber scow tied up at Buffalo. The men piled onto the two vessels and crossed the river, reaching the Canadian side at 1:30 on the morning of June 1. After landing about a mile below Fort Erie, they moved northward to the hamlet of Lower Ferry, where they quickly gained control. After posting some men to guard the place, the main body of Starr's force turned back south to Fort Erie.

They reached the town of about one hundred inhabitants shortly before dawn and quickly captured the half-dozen members of the Royal Canadian Rifles stationed there primarily to stop deserters from crossing into the United States. They also cut the telegraph lines, but not before Robert Larmour, the assistant route superintendent with the Buffalo & Lake Huron Railway, telegraphed Major General George Napier, British military commander of the Canadas, that the Fenians had arrived. Larmour then loaded a train with some valuable railway equipment and headed for Port

Colborne, with some Fenians in pursuit on a handcar. They did not catch him, but they did tear up the rails and set fire to Sauerwein's bridge east of Ridgeway in an attempt to stop any troop movement between Port Colborne and Fort Erie.

Meanwhile, General John O'Neill had crossed into Canada with about one thousand Fenian men. O'Neill was thirty-two, had immigrated to the United States as a child, and served in the Union Army during the Civil War. Tall and handsome, there was no doubting O'Neill's bravery or his ability as a soldier, but his ambition seems to have exceeded his ability; when he did not advance through the Union ranks quickly enough, he transferred to a black regiment in order to be promoted to captain. He was totally devoted to the Fenian cause.

O'Neill's men reached Lower Ferry around the same time Starr's contingent moved into Fort Erie. About one hundred were sent northward to guard the Niagara Road and stop any incursions from Chippawa. The rest of Fenians then made their way to Fort Erie.

Residents of the town were in a panic. Some, giving credence to the rumours, had already fled. Many went to Buffalo, where, they sensibly reasoned, they would be safe from any Fenian attacks. A number gathered in the house belonging to the U.S. consul in Fort Erie, identified by a large American flag. Others sounded the alarm. Twenty-two-year-old Sam Johnston, who had fought with the Union Army during the American Civil War, borrowed the finest horse he could locate and rode through the countryside announcing the arrival of the invaders. And, at one point early in the morning, a customs officer could be heard shouting that the Fenians had arrived and were killing everyone they encountered.

Nothing was further from the truth. When O'Neill and his men reached Fort Erie, they rounded up the men of the village and had them listen to a proclamation which declared their quarrel was with the British, not Canadian civilians, and that they would not harm the populace. Then the men were sent home under house arrest. The townsfolk were required to provide breakfast rations for one thousand invaders, and to turn over tools, livestock, and horses, but were otherwise unharmed. Some, in fact, were able to leave even after the invaders arrived, as the ferry continued to run between Fort Erie and the American side for several hours on June 1, taking frightened Canadians to safety and bringing back Fenians who had managed to elude American authorities. Others made their way to join O'Neill's force in boats and barges, but even as they arrived, large numbers of their brothers-in-arms were deserting. The U.S. gunboat *Michigan* was clearly visible in the Niagara River, suggesting it was only a matter of time before government action of some variety was aimed at the Fenians.

Nevertheless, O'Neill continued with his plans. After securing Fort Erie, he and his men moved northward to Frenchman's Creek, where they could watch for the arrival of any British-Canadian troops from the direction of Lake Ontario.

Canada under Attack

* * *

On the afternoon of May 31, Colonel Patrick L. MacDougall ordered a battalion to go to Fort Erie. The invasion had not yet begun, but MacDougall, the British army officer who had command of the Canadian militia, had become convinced that there was some truth to the rumours of an imminent attack. By six o'clock that evening, the Queen's Own Rifles (QOR) of Toronto got word that four hundred men were to head for Niagara. Hamilton's Thirteenth Battalion was also called up.

It had been more than half a century since the War of 1812. Much of the memory of those times had faded, but a myth had begun to take root — the myth that the Canadian militia had been largely responsible for the successful defence of the province against invading Americans. In fact, British regulars and native allies played key roles in repelling the enemy. Although the militia had also been called up during the Rebellions of 1837, relatively few had actually dealt with the insurgents. Yet, after nearly thirty years of peace, much of the public and most of the militia firmly believed that they could deal with any invader.

In fact, although militia members did receive some training in the use of weapons, shortages of weapons and ammunition were an ongoing problem. What shooting practice most militia men did receive was inadequate, especially against a force such as the Fenians — battle-hardened veterans from the American Civil War. To a great extent, the militia functioned as a social club, one that provided opportunities for upwardly mobile young men to make contacts with others in the community, including businessmen, professionals, and politicians. The associations often proved invaluable to budding careers. If an individual could also present himself as a high-ranking militia officer, his status in the community was greatly enhanced.

As it happened, the commanders of both the Toronto and Hamilton contingents were ambitious and successful citizen-soldiers who had some theoretical knowledge of military tactics, some training, some understanding of how the militia bureaucracy worked, and absolutely no experience in battle.

Lieutenant-Colonel John Stoughton Dennis was forty-six and a wealthy land surveyor with a family history of military service. Dennis had risen through the militia ranks to become brigade major of the Fifth Militia Military District. He liked to call attention to himself and was notable for the lavish sidewhiskers that flowed from his sideburns, down the side of his face, to the top of his chest. He was also determined to make a name for himself as a military man, and so, when he got word that the Queen's Own Rifles was being called up for active duty, he asked for and received permission to replace their commander, Major Charles T. Gillmor. Tactically, it was not the best move, since the men were not accustomed to serving under him. It did not do much for morale, either, as the young men of the QOR resented losing their popular commander.

Still, there was a great deal of excitement about the possibility of fighting the Fenians. Most of the Queen's Own Rifles were young and many were University of Toronto students. Dennis's orders were to have them board the steamer *City of Toronto* early in the morning on June 1, cross to Port Dalhousie, at the northern terminus of the Welland Canal, then travel by rail to Port Colborne on Lake Erie, where the Welland Field Battery had been called up to defend the southern end of the Welland Canal. Dennis was instructed to await further orders there. Although initial plans called for 400 men to sail from Toronto, only 356 were aboard the *City of Toronto* when she set out around 6:30 a.m. However, another 125 men followed that afternoon.

Meanwhile, militia in Hamilton were receiving orders of their own. Members of the Hamilton Volunteer Thirteenth Infantry Battalion were told to report to the drill shed on James Street by six o'clock that same morning. They were commanded by forty-two-year-old Alfred Booker, an English immigrant and successful businessman who ran an auction house. Clever and well-spoken, Booker had plenty of experience with the militia and the red tape involved in its running. During the American Civil War he had been liaison officer with the British military. Like Dennis, he also lacked real military experience, although he had commanded several volunteer units patrolling the Niagara frontier in 1864, following the St. Albans raid. Now he hoped to make a name for himself defending Canada West against the invading Fenians.

The Hamilton contingent set out on the Great Western Railway at 9 a.m., headed for Dunnville, situated on the Grand River upstream from Lake Erie. In Caledonia, they picked up members of two Haldimand County militia companies, the Caledonia and York Rifles. The circuitous route the train took brought them to Dunnville by four that afternoon.

As the Canadian militia companies were making their preparations, the British army was also alerted to the threat. George Napier, military commander for Canada West, appointed Lieutenant-Colonel George J. Peacocke commander-in-chief for Niagara defence. Peacocke was a consummate professional who was stationed in Hamilton; he was arguably far more competent than his superior officer, who failed to provide any orders for action. It was some time before Napier bothered to direct Peacocke to proceed to St. Catharines and take whatever action he felt was required.

At 2 p.m. on June 1, long after the Hamilton and Toronto contingents had set out for the Niagara Peninsula, Peacocke headed out. By 9 p.m. he was at Chippawa, where he telegraphed Booker in Dunnville and told him to rendez-vous with Dennis in Port Colborne.

Earlier that day, the Fenians had sent scouts as far as Black Creek, north of Frenchman's Creek, where they encountered a small body of mounted men. Their presence, and a brief exchange of gunfire, was enough to push the Fenians back to Frenchman's Creek. Peacocke was duly advised of events, but, possibly because of the inadequate maps with which the British-Canadian defenders were supplied, came to the conclusion that the main Fenian force was at Black Creek. Based on this, he developed a plan to have the forces from Port Colborne meet him at Stevensville, thirteen kilometres south of Chippawa, between ten and eleven the next day. By that time, reinforcements Peacocke was counting on should have arrived and would accompany him. In addition, Dennis was to board the steam ferry *International*, get on the Niagara River, and prevent Fenians from returning to the American side as the remainder of the British-Canadian forces routed them. The outlines of the plan were telegraphed to Port Colborne, but to make sure the details were clearly understood by Dennis and Booker, Peacocke dispatched Captain Charles Akers of the Royal Engineers to personally explain things to the militia commanders. Akers set off around midnight and Peacocke advised Dennis by telegraph that he could expect him to arrive around 1:30 in the morning of June 2.

About the same time as Akers was setting out, Booker and his troops reached Port Colborne. Like Dennis, Booker was a lieutenant-colonel, but had been promoted to that rank shortly before Dennis, and so technically outranked him. Booker's first action on reaching Port Colborne was to relieve Dennis of his command and put himself in charge of both the Queen's Own Rifles and the Hamilton Battalion, along with the supporting troops. As a result, Dennis saw his chances of military glory fading rapidly, especially when the *International* ferryboat failed to arrive. The ferry had put into port in Buffalo rather than risk damage at the hands of the Fenians.

It looked as if Dennis would have to follow Booker in whatever action he took. Then Dennis hit on the idea of enlisting the *W. T. Robb*, a converted tug owned by business-man Lachlan McCallum of Stromness, east of Dunnville. McCallum, who had been watching Fenian activities for some time, was head of the Dunnville Naval Brigade and as early as April 1865 had offered to put the *Robb* at the disposal of the government for defence against the Fenians. Now Dennis telegraphed him, asking that the *Robb* come to Port Colborne, along with the Dunnville Naval Brigade. By add-ing the men of the Welland Field Battery, who had gathered in Port Colborne, Dennis would have a respectable body of defenders to attack the Fenians from the Niagara River.

As June 1 faded into June 2, the two lieutenant-col-onels discussed strategy, aided by input from railwayman Robert Larmour, and from Charles Clarke, an agent with McMicken's secret service. During the day, a number of curi-ous individuals had visited the Fenian encampment with lit-tle interference from the invaders. Among them was the Fort Erie customs collector, who had accompanied Larmour to Port Colborne, and who reported that most of the Fenians he

John O'Neill

had seen were drunk, and that they could easily be defeated by four hundred men. Charles Clarke more or less confirmed Graham's report, estimating that there were perhaps 450 Fenians in camp, but warned that another 200 reinforcements were expected to join them around 3 a.m.

Based on that information, and to no small extent influenced by his personal ambitions, Booker decided to head for Fort Erie, where he expected to meet the Fenians. When the telegram advising Peacocke of this new plan reached the commander he opposed the idea, but rather than advise of his disapproval by return telegram he decided Akers could straighten things out when he reached Port Colborne.

Akers did begin by repeating the original orders Peacocke had given. Booker and Dennis were to rendezvous with him in Stevensville. But the two lieutenant-colonels convinced Akers that the intelligence they had received from Graham and Clarke was more current and more accurate than anything Peacocke had and persuaded Akers to back their plan. Booker would take his troops part way by rail — the track and Sauerwein's bridge east of Ridgeway having been repaired — then march towards Fort Erie and the Fenians, while Dennis took the *Robb* along Lake Erie and down the Niagara River. Peacocke could adhere to much of his original plan, marching from Chippawa southward in the direction of Stevensville and, beyond that, Fort Erie.

At three in the morning, the revised plan was telegraphed to Peacocke. An hour later, the *Robb* reached Port Colborne with Dennis in command of the troops on board. Accompanied by Akers, he got the men of Welland Field Battery aboard. It would have been helpful if they had been accompanied by their big guns, four 9-pound rifled, breechloading Armstrongs, as the men had received artillery training with them and could have put them to good use against the enemy. Two of the guns had been stored in Port Colborne and two in Port Robinson until early 1866, when a lieutenant-colonel in the British army had learned that the guns were unguarded. They had been moved to Hamilton, and there they remained while the Welland Field Battery prepared to defend their country as infantry.

Booker, in the meantime, was supposed to wait for Peacocke's reply. But he was growing increasingly impatient.

At 5 a.m, he had the men of the Queen's Own Rifles, the Hamilton Thirteenth, and the York and Caledonia rifle companies board nine railway flat cars and start out in the direction of Fort Erie. Twenty minutes later, the telegram from Peacocke arrived.

Booker had 841 officers and men at his command: 481 from the Queen's Own Rifles, 265 from Hamilton's Thirteenth Battalion, 48 from the Caledonia Rifle Company, and 47 from the York Rifle Company. The militia's initial enthusiasm at the prospect of seeing some action was being undermined by some preventable hardships. Many of the men were inadequately supplied, lacking tents, blankets, and basic tools. A number had no knapsacks or canteens. Many had not eaten since the night before, while others had managed nothing more than an early breakfast before setting out for the Niagara Peninsula. On the morning of June 2, there was hardly any food to be found in Port Colborne with which to feed the men, although a number were supplied with dry crackers and salt fish. Within a short time, they were suffering from a raging thirst, but unable to quench it because they had not been supplied with water or containers in which to carry it.

Added to hunger and thirst were problems with the weapons and ammunition. The Fenians were also better armed, trained, and experienced than the defenders. While the Fenians had more rifles than they could use and, after their Civil War service, were comfortable with their weapons, many of the militia had to make do with guns that were either unfamiliar or obsolete. Half of the Welland Field Battery carried long Enfield rifles, but the other half had been given Enfield muskets, which the British army had stopped using thirteen years prior. Most of the men under Booker had muzzle-loading Enfields, but were inadequately supplied with ammunition. Standard military practice dictated that an infantryman going into battle should have between forty and sixty rounds of ammunition. Most of the men of the Queen's Own Rifles were initially given just five rounds. Although Booker later augmented this with another thirty rounds, they were still undersupplied. So were the forty-nine men of the Rifles' Company Five who were armed with modern seven-shot repeating Spencer rifles. These required special ammunition, of which the men were given just twenty-eight rounds. Making matters worse, although most of the militia had participated in rifle drills, about half of them had never actually fired their weapons at all. And the majority of the men under Booker's command were very young. At least half the militia from Hamilton and Toronto were under twenty, many of the latter fresh from finishing the school year at the University of Toronto. Some of the volunteers were as young as fifteen.

If Booker gave any thought to the youth and inexperience of the men under his command, there was no evidence of it on the morning of June 2. Booker and his trainload of troops reached Ridgeway at 6 a.m. A short time later, Sam Johnston reported to him. After riding hard to give the alarm about the invaders, Johnston had followed the Fenians and now advised Booker that they were about five kilometres north of the village. He estimated their numbers at fifteen hundred, armed with rifles, but no artillery. A small number of the Fenians were mounted on horses they had liberated from the civilians of the district, but they had no saddles and nothing resembling a cavalry. Neither did the defenders, for that matter. Booker was the only one on horseback, and his mount had been borrowed from the only other officer who had bothered to bring a horse, Major James Skinner of Hamilton.

* * *

Long before Booker and Dennis concocted their plan to meet the Fenians, John O'Neill set into motion a plan of his own. Through a combination of his own military experience and good intelligence — possibly from tapping telegraph lines — O'Neill realized that the British-Canadians would most likely move against him from Chippawa and Port Colborne. Realizing he would be greatly outnumbered, he decided his best strategy was to meet the force proceeding from Port Colborne and engage it before it connected with Peacocke and his reinforcements. Unlike the defenders, who were working with inadequate and obsolete maps, the Fenians knew the territory well and had almost certainly sent scouts into the area in the weeks leading up to the invasion. Just north of Ridgeway, the limestone ridge that gave the town its name was the main feature of the countryside. It was a perfect location to do battle. Because of the elevation, visibility was excellent. The Fenians would see the defenders coming from miles away and yet remain hidden behind trees and shrubbery.

Less than two years earlier, Booker had been stationed in the Niagara Peninsula, yet it seems he was largely unfamiliar with this terrain. Or perhaps he simply choose to ignore the Fenians' geographic advantage. He certainly seemed determined to engage the enemy, even though the orders to rendezvous with Peacocke were still in force. Five minutes after Booker boarded the train in Port Colborne, a telegram from Peacocke had arrived. It explained that he would be leaving later than expected, and that Booker should tailor his schedule accordingly. Given the importance of the message, a railway employee was sent after Booker and caught up with him south of Ridgeway, about five minutes after the Canadians spotted the Fenian force.

At the subsequent military inquiry, Booker would insist that he did not receive the message until 9:30 that morning. But other evidence strongly suggests that the telegram reached him at 7:30 and he deliberately chose to ignore it. He led his men into battle.

Chapter 5
Ridgeway and Fort Erie

June 2 was a lovely late spring morning in the Niagara countryside. As Booker and his soldiers moved northward, they saw fields of grain, an apple orchard, and woodlots stretch before them. There were also wooden rail fences, testimony to generations of peaceful settlement in the district. But a close observer could see that preparations had been made for war. Using tools confiscated from the residents of Fort Erie, the Fenians had built bullet shields from some fences. They were barely visible to the approaching Canadians, who could just make out the tops of the enemy heads and, flying proudly above them, several green flags emblazoned with golden sunbursts.

Company Five of the Queen's Own Rifles, dressed in green uniforms and carrying their state-of-the-art Spencer rifles, formed the advance guard. According to one of them, fifteen-year-old Fred McCallum, they were in a wheatfield when the Fenians opened fire. In early June, long before the wheat had achieved its full height, the Canadians were an easy target. As the shooting started, they hurried to take cover behind a snake fence and return fire.

Ensign Malcolm McEachern was among them. Born in Scotland, he was thirty-five, a store manager and Methodist Sunday School teacher in Toronto, as well as father of five. A good shot, he thought he could improve his accuracy by pulling one of the rails off the fence. As he did so, a Fenian bullet caught him in the abdomen. "I am shot!" he cried as he went down. Taken to a nearby cabin, he died twenty minutes later, the first casualty of the day.

The battle raged for two hours. At first the Canadians seemed to be gaining ground. They continued to move steadily forward, apparently driving the Fenians back towards the north. But their progress was an illusion. O'Neill had kept the main body of his force in reserve, sending only skirmishers forward to meet the Canadians. While the militia fought bravely, earning some respect from their enemy, it was all too apparent to the battle-seasoned invaders that the Canadians were green troops who unnecessarily exposed themselves to gunfire.

At one point, with Canadians on both sides of his men,

O'Neill was forced to pull back a short distance and regroup. Booker had been gradually sending more and more men into the field, until, around 9:30, he deployed the last of the Thirteenth Battalion. In the confusion of battle, a number of the Canadians concluded that these red-coated men were newly arrived British reinforcements. A cheer went up.

Soon afterward, things began to go very wrong.

Exactly what happened next and in what order has never been fully understood, despite the accounts of participants in the battle. It appears that some of the Canadians caught sight of Fenians on horseback and concluded cavalry was present. That information spread quickly across the battlefield. Orders were given to "form square" — the correct manoeuvre for infantry about to engage men on horseback. But standing in a tightly packed block only made the Canadians more vulnerable to enemy fire. Booker ordered them to regroup, which they attempted to do as the Fenians kept up their lethal fire. But, in their effort to follow orders, the men who had formed the square ran into other Canadians, creating widespread confusion. At that point, Booker apparently gave the order to retire. Or perhaps not. Some of those who were present at the Battle of Ridgeway later claimed the order to retire was given before anyone reported seeing cavalry.

Whatever the truth, there is no disputing that Booker's lack of experience, as well as that of his men, created mayhem. Many of the militiamen confused the order to retire with a command to retreat, which turned into a panicked run for safety. The Fenians followed, chasing the main body of the troops all the way back to Ridgeway. There, the Canadians followed the railway tracks, heading for Port Colborne.

News of the defeat spread by word-of-mouth and by telegraph. As the wounded and dead were gathered and tended to, the extent of the Canadians' loss was calculated. Seven members of the Queen's Own Rifles had been killed: Ensign Malcolm McEachren, Privates William Smith, Mark Defries, Christopher Alderson, William Fairbanks Tempest, John Harriman Mewburn, and Malcolm McKenzie. Two more, Corporal Francis Lackey and Sergeant Hugh Matheson, would die within two days. They were among the twenty-eight men were wounded: twenty from the Rifles, six from Hamilton's Thirteenth Battalion, and two from the York Rifle Company. Others would also eventually die from their wounds.

As many as eight Fenians were killed, and ten wounded. They had been ridiculed and seriously underestimated, but they had won their first battle with Canadian forces. And they were not done yet. After some minimal looting in the village of Ridgeway, they turned back towards Fort Erie, where another battle awaited.

* * *

Peacocke's original plan had been for Dennis and some men to board the *International* and get onto the Niagara

River. When the ferry failed to show up, Booker recalled meeting Lachlan McCallum in Dunnville. Originally from Tyree, Scotland, McCallum had immigrated to Canada as a young man. He started building a fortune by selling wood during the construction of the Feeder Canal, which diverted water from the Grand River to the Welland Canal. In time he owned a number of businesses, including a boatyard and general store, and was also deeply involved in politics.

McCallum was captain of the Dunnville Naval Brigade, which he had formed in 1863 and had dressed in blue uniforms with silver buttons. When Dennis telegraphed him asking for the *Robb* as a substitute for the *International* ferryboat, McCallum did not hesitate for an instant. He loaded his men into the boat, one of the fastest on Lake Erie, and headed for Port Colborne. There Dennis boarded, along with Captain Akers, who was serving as his second-in-command, and the men of the Welland Field Battery. Not counting these two officers, there were 107 men aboard: three officers and fifty-nine men from the Welland Battery, three officers and forty-three men from the Dunnville Naval Brigade.

When she set out from Port Colborne towards the Niagara River, the 128-foot *Robb* steamed through dense fog. As the sun rose the fog burned away, leaving the men sailing through clear, calm weather. When they reached the river, they discovered a crowd of spectators had gathered on the American shore, eager to see any action that might take place. The men were ordered below, out of concern that the sight of armed men in uniform might draw unnecessary attention from American authorities, as well as alert Fenians to their presence.

American officials certainly were watching the progress of the *Robb*. The boat was stopped by a revenue cutter and the leaders were asked to explain their business. Their response was sufficiently satisfactory for the captain of the gunboat to inform them that the Fenians had been in the area but had abandoned the Newbigging farm, north of Fort Erie.

A short time later, the *Robb* docked at the town and Dennis sent the men ashore. Fort Erie seemed deserted, with none of the bustle that was common in the harbour. Telegraph wires, which the Fenians had cut the previous day, lay strewn on the ground. A search of the town turned up a number of suspicious individuals, eleven of whom were taken prisoner and locked up in the town hall. Then Dennis sent two parties of about three dozen men each to search the countryside north and west of the village and take into custody any Fenians they encountered.

They roamed as far north as Black Creek before returning to Fort Erie. Once there, all the prisoners they had taken were put aboard the *Robb*. Peacocke had still not shown up and Dennis came to the conclusion that he had not accepted the revised plan. Dennis decided he had best return to Port Colborne. Rather than transport the prisoners, he made up his mind to leave them at Fort Erie, with several men to guard them. Captain Richard Sylvester King, a physician and commander of the Welland Field Battery, objected, pointing out there were more prisoners than guards, but was overruled.

By this time, some of the townsfolk who had been in hiding were emerging or returning from the countryside. As they did, word was relayed to Dennis that Booker had met the Fenians in battle and had been defeated. Other people told basically the same story, but Dennis and some of the other officers refused to believe it. It seemed to them inconceivable that the Fenians — disorganized, drunken Irishmen who had been easily repelled in New Brunswick — could get the better of British-Canadian troops. Especially if, as some of the intelligence indicated, desertions had dwindled the Fenian ranks to the point where the defenders had a distinct advantage. Dennis would not even take the word of Lewis Palmer, a septuagenarian who had been a British soldier in the War of 1812. Palmer had also witnessed the events of the Rebellions of 1837, and, from the front porch of his house, two miles west of Fort Erie, he had personally seen the main body of Fenians on their way back to the town. Quickly mounting his horse, he had ridden through the streets, sounding a warning. He could not reach Dennis, but did speak to Captain King. Soon afterwards, his report was corroborated by others who had seen the Fenians on the move. Although there was some dispute as to just how many Fenians were marching eastward, there was by now little doubt where they were heading.

Meanwhile, Captain Akers, having heard reports of the

Fenians' approach, had climbed a ladder on the side of the railway terminal to get a better look. What he saw convinced him that an attack was imminent, but, rather than report to Dennis and assist in preparing to meet the invaders, he got into a buggy and headed for Port Colborne along a quiet lakeshore road.

Dennis was finally persuaded that the Fenians were, indeed, moving towards him and his men. But he thought the threat was minimal, apparently certain that this was not a victorious army of four or five hundred, but only a group of a hundred or so stragglers who were probably more interested in getting back to the American shore than in anything else. Confident the men under his command could defeat them, he ordered the Welland Field Battery ashore. Old Palmer, who estimated the main Fenian force at around eight hundred, was adamant that there were not enough men to defeat the invaders. The best thing Dennis could do, he argued, was get his men aboard the *Robb* and take it out to the middle of the Niagara River. At first, Dennis seemed willing to follow the advice, especially since Captain King was also warning him of the danger to the men and Captain Akers was nowhere to be found. Dennis had most of the Welland Field Battery and the Dunnville Naval Brigade board the boat. And then he changed his mind and ordered them back ashore, where they assembled in two lines.

The Fenians were on higher ground as they came along Garrison Road, which ran into the main street of Fort Erie

Battle of Ridgeway

parallel to the waterfront, with the river to the east and a row of houses to the west. As soon as the Fenians reached the main street, Captain McCallum gave the order to fire. Dennis overruled him. Then the Fenians began shooting at the Canadians, who returned their fire immediately. When he heard the first shots, Dennis reacted instinctively: he ducked and ran for cover. McCallum shouted after him, "Where the hell are you going?" In seconds, Dennis was out of sight.

There was also an interchange of fire between the Fenians and the men aboard the *Robb*. Realizing the boat was in considerable danger, the *Robb*'s captain decided the safest course of action was to move it into the middle of the river, which he did, and then slowly sailed downstream.

Greatly outnumbered, the Canadians could not stand their ground for long. McCallum ordered his men to fire as they saw fit. What ensued was a street battle, with members of the Welland Field Battery and the Dunnville Naval Brigade taking cover near buildings and firing at the Fenians, while spectators watched from the American shore, cheering the Fenians.

A number of Canadians were captured, but several others were able to move north along Front Street and take shelter in a house owned by George Lewis. From inside, they continued firing at the Fenians, dodging bullets that ripped through the wooden walls and windows. Miraculously, although the place was riddled with bullet holes, none of the men inside was hurt.

But it was only a matter of time until they ran out of ammunition. When it became apparent the Canadians were unable to continue the fight, the Fenians insisted that they surrender. There were grumblings that they would be shot, but General John O'Neill would have none of this. His policy, right from the start, was to treat civilians and prisoners as humanely as possible. Even so, the men inside the Lewis house were unwilling to submit. They stood their ground until Lieutenant Angus MacDonald handed a white hand-kerchief to Abram Thewlis, Lachlan McCallum's brother-in-law, and told him to surrender. As he was doing so, the men in the house made their escape through the back door and eventually reached the river, where they were taken aboard the *Robb*.

For the men involved, it probably seemed the fighting took forever. In fact, it was all over in an hour. For the invaders the casualties were higher than at Ridgeway. Fourteen Fenians were killed, including one who was bayoneted. A number of Canadians were wounded, but none lost their lives, although it was a close call for Dr. King, who had his foot shot off and bled profusely. Cared for by an American doctor in Buffalo, he lost part of his leg but survived.

The Canadians captured at Fort Erie, along with those taken at Ridgeway, were housed in the reeve's residence, which had been taken over as O'Neill's temporary headquarters. Meanwhile, the *Robb* made her way to the lake under heavy fire from Fenians along the shore. Amazingly, the only damage was to the boat, which returned to Port Colborne.

* * *

Although he was commander-in-chief of the Niagara operation, Peacocke had missed all the day's action. Setting off from Chippawa at seven that morning, he had marched towards Stevensville by the longest route possible. Two other courses were rejected. One, which could have been covered partly by train, because of the threat of ambush, the second because the road might not have been ideal for moving artillery. Peacocke's progress was slow and agonizing for the British regulars, who carried sixty pounds of equipment and dressed in heavy greatcoats. As the morning progressed and the temperature climbed, they became desperately thirsty and some collapsed of heat exhaustion. One, Corporal Carrington, died. Around noon, just short of Stevensville, Peacocke stopped his men after learning that Booker had been defeated at Ridgeway. They spent the afternoon hours resting in the shade of some trees.

Around four in the afternoon, Peacocke learned that the Fenians were returning to the Niagara River and decided it was time to move. It took ninety minutes to get the men ready. Just before they began the march eastward, reinforcements arrived, in the shape of fifty-five cavalrymen from the Governor General's Body Guard under Major George Taylor Denison. The mounted soldiers set out ahead of Peacocke's column, keeping an eye out for Fenians. At one point they spotted two men climbing a fence, carrying rifles similar to those with which the Fenians were armed. They shot, hitting both men, who turned out to be local farmers who had picked up the weapons after Ridgeway. One of them later died of his wounds.

As darkness neared, Peacocke worried they might encounter Fenians. To avoid attracting their attention, he ordered his men not to light fires. They spent a short, restless night in the open and were wakened at 4:30 a.m. when a supply wagon arrived with beef and bread. A little later, Denison, who had been sent ahead to scout, heard that between two and three thousand Fenian reinforcements from Buffalo were massing at the site of the War of 1812 fort, south of town. It was not true, but he was not aware of this at first. When he got to the Niagara River he spotted a barge full of Fenians, apparently waiting to cross over to Canada. After sending word to Peacocke, who halted his troops, Denison talked to the captain of the U.S. revenue cutter *Michigan*, who explained that the men on the barge were actually retreating from Canada but had been stopped by American authorities.

Once he had this information, Peacocke resumed his march to Fort Erie. Denison, meanwhile, arrived there around six in the morning and freed the Canadian prisoners who had been taken at Ridgeway and the skirmish in the town.

* * *

O'Neill had brought his men to the old fort, but it soon became clear that he would not be able to hold the place against British-Canadian defenders. He was down to about seven hundred men. Although there were reports that several hundred reinforcements were waiting on the American side, U.S. officials would not allow them to cross into Canada. Meanwhile, approximately three thousand hostile regular soldiers and militia were within a short march of O'Neill's temporary headquarters. The men might have tried the same tactic that worked at Ridgeway — engaging a smaller contingent if the opportunity arose — but in the meantime they had to eat, and, with thousands of soldiers now in the Peninsula, acquiring food undetected would be difficult. O'Neill was prepared to remain and fight to the very end, but his officers overruled him. Late that night, in barges towed by tugs, the Fenians headed back to the American side. Around 2 a.m. on June 3, they were intercepted by the U.S. government boat *Harrison*, which alerted the *Michigan*. O'Neill and his officers were taken aboard, while the rest of the Fenians were taken to Black Rock and kept aboard the barges until officials could deal with them. These were the men Denison had seen when he reached the Niagara River.

It was not the strangest ruins the young officer encountered that day. Very early that morning, while most of Peacocke's men and the reinforcements slept, Denison had been awake, inspecting the camp. Out of the darkness a figure called out, "Is that you, George?"

The man drew nearer. Denison saw he was wearing working clothes, with a cap pulled down low on his head and a scarf wound around his neck. He also sported a heavy mustache and, as Denison would later write, "had a wild, hunted look about the eyes." The stranger asked Denison if he recognized him, and at first the younger man did not. Then the voice twigged his memory and he realized that he was speaking to Lieutenant-Colonel Dennis.

After fleeing from the skirmish at Fort Erie, Dennis had

taken shelter in a hayloft and waited there for several hours. When the coast was clear, he made his way to a friend's home, where he shaved off his highly recognizable side whiskers and disguised himself as a labourer. He had come to Peacocke's encampment to give his report — but without knowing anything of the outcome of the day's fighting at Fort Erie.

Chapter 6
Quebec and Repercussions

The Fenian threat in Niagara ended when the invaders crossed the river to Buffalo in the early morning hours of Sunday, June 3. At this point, however, Canadian authorities could not predict what might happen next, especially with an estimated five thousand Fenians still gathered in Buffalo, so they continued to send troops to flood the area. Booker was ordered to take the Thirteenth Battalion to Fort Erie. By the time he arrived, a British-Canadian force of three thousand was nearby, with more ready to provide reinforcements.

While the American government was silent about the

raids, action was taken to deter the Fenians. On June 3, Major General George Meade, who had been instrumental in controlling the invasion in New Brunswick, instructed General William Barry of Buffalo to be sure neutrality laws were strictly enforced. Although Barry had only eight hundred men at his disposal, those Fenians — whose numbers were probably nowhere near the estimated five thousand — seemed to have lost interest. Barry was able to make arrests or seize weapons whenever it appeared more trouble was brewing. However, it was not until June 6 that an official American declaration against the Fenian incursion was issued.

Ironically, the very next day, the Fenians invaded Quebec.

The Fenians had envisioned a concerted raid on the United Province of Canada, an attack targeting Hamilton, Toronto, and Montreal, which would bring the government to its knees. Partly from a lack of organization, and partly because of the efforts of Canadian and American authorities, the plan fell through. The Fenians had, however, gathered along the New York and Vermont borders, ready to attack Canada. While they must have been greatly encouraged by the news from Ridgeway, the action there worked to their disadvantage, as the military in Canada East was now fully prepared for the possibility of an attack.

The Richelieu River had historically been an important route for would-be invaders. Most of the defence preparations were concentrated west of the Richelieu, leaving other areas vulnerable to the invaders. Among these was Missisquoi County, just across the border from St. Albans, Vermont.

Somewhere between fifteen hundred and two thousand Fenians gathered there, ready to cross the border into Canada. They were commanded by General Samuel P. Spears, a graduate of West Point. But ammunition was slow to arrive, partly because American authorities were making greater efforts to enforce neutrality laws. In addition, only about a thousand Fenians were ready to follow Spears into battle.

Meanwhile, reports of Fenians gathering elsewhere along the border, plus the activities of British regulars and the militia, had provoked numerous rumours. Many people fled their homes in fear of attack. So, when Spears finally crossed the border on June 7, there was little initial resistance. By this time, the Fenians had been waiting for action for some time and were short of supplies. Hungry and impatient, they looted houses, for both food and booty.

Spears captured the three communities of St. Armand, Stanbridge East, and Frelighsburg, and established their headquarters at Pigeon Hill, about seventy kilometres southeast of Montreal. In a repeat of what had happened at Campobello, a small group of Fenians captured the flag atop the customs house in Frelighsburg. This was later displayed as a prize of war in the United States, but in fact the Fenians had little to celebrate. On June 9, most of them withdrew across the border. A couple of hundred were involved in a brief skirmish at Pigeon Hill, but it was no contest. The Canadian defenders, whose weapons included some Armstrong guns, easily routed the invaders, who were chased back to the border by the Royal Troop of Guides. Sixteen prisoners were taken in Canada, while a number of Fenians were arrested on their return to the U.S.

The military suffered no casualties, but even after the Fenians were repelled communities close to the border remained on high alert, with at least one tragic result.

A group of Royal Welch Fusiliers was on guard near Eccles Hill on the night of June 10, when a picket spotted someone walking along the road. The person was ordered to halt and identify himself. There was no response, and then the stranger began to run. All seven members of the picket fired, instantly killing seventy-one-year-old Margaret Vincent. The elderly woman, who was quite deaf, had been on her way to get water from a well, probably did not hear the command to stop, and took fright when she spotted the armed men. The accident horrified residents, who erected a small memorial in Vincent's memory.

* * *

For many Canadians, the events of early June 1866 seemed unbelievable. After years of looking at the Fenians as comical, inept drunkards, it seemed impossible that the defenders of Canada had been defeated not once, but twice, on the same day. Fears that much worse was to come resulted in the suspension of *habeas corpus* on June 8. Discrimination against Irish Catholics flared up, although John A. Macdonald, D'Arcy McGee, and others did what they could to control a serious backlash.

Recriminations flew elsewhere, notably among the men who saw action at Ridgeway. Booker was criticized for his order to retire, with many of the militia convinced that they would have won the day if they been allowed to remain on the field. They did not seem to grasp that the success achieved in the early part of the battle had been against a fraction of O'Neill's forces, and had they remained on the field a bloodbath might have followed. The Queen's Own Rifles and the Thirteenth Battalion, playing out the rivalry between Hamilton and Toronto that exists to this day, lobbed insults at each other. Referring to the colour of their uniforms, the Rifles called the men of the Thirteenth "Scarlet Runners," while the men of the Thirteenth insisted that the Rifles' initials, QOR, stood for "Quickest Outta Ridgeway."

Then there were pressing questions that needed to be answered. Why had Booker disobeyed Peacocke's orders in favour of his own scheme? Was the defeat at Ridgeway a direct result of his incompetence, or did it have more to do with the militia's lack of training and provisions? Was Dennis guilty of cowardice, given his abandonment of his men at Fort Erie? Eventually, two military inquiries would investigate, but their conclusions were unsatisfactory as

Eccles Hill — First Invasion of Quebec

far as many Canadians were concerned. Accused by other officers of endangering his men and deserting them under enemy fire, Stoughton Dennis demanded an inquiry. It was presided over by none other than George Denison, the officer Dennis had first encountered when he sought out Peacocke. Dennis was completely exonerated, even though Denison himself believed he was guilty of disobeying orders. Dennis later went to Manitoba where he returned to his work as a surveyor. In 1871, he became Canada's first surveyor general and was later appointed deputy minister of the interior.

Alfred Booker also demanded a court of inquiry. It, too, was presided over by George Denison. Like Dennis,

Booker was exonerated. Denison actually praised him for his bravery, but some of the officers who had served under him were unhappy with the outcome. They engineered a smear campaign, hiring Alexander Somerville, who freelanced for a Hamilton newspaper, the *Spectator,* to write a book criticizing his actions at Ridgeway. Nevertheless, when Booker resigned from the militia in 1867, he was allowed to retain his rank, signalling that the Canadian government was satisfied with his service. He moved to Montreal, where he ran a business until his death in 1871.

For the general public, it took some time to come to grips with the events at Ridgeway and to mourn the dead. There was considerable comment about what had happened, including discussion of what should be done with the eighty-one Fenian prisoners who had been captured, sixty-five in Canada West and the remainder in Canada East. D'Arcy McGee, always outspoken when it came to the Fenians, was adamant — it was imperative that they feel the full weight of the law. As far as he was concerned, they were "an aggregate of individual murderers banded together for wholesale murder." Writing to Lord John Wodehouse, the Lord Lieutenant of Ireland, McGee said, "Some example must be made here, but our intention is to inflict only the minimum of capital punishment, sentencing the rank and file to hard labour." Most of the Canadian cabinet agreed with him.

For some time, McGee's attitude towards the Fenians and their campaign to free Ireland from British rule had

87

caused him considerable trouble. After Ridgeway and his outspoken condemnation of the invaders, hatred of McGee rose to new heights. In August 1866, stones were thrown at him while he walked along a Montreal street. At a meeting in Pointe-Saint-Charles, a district of Montreal, hostile members of the audience made so much noise that his speech could not be heard. He was accused of condemning the Fenians in an effort to win votes in the 1866 election of the Legislative Assembly, although among some Irish Canadians his comments had exactly the opposite effect. During the campaign, his headquarters was attacked by a violent mob, who might well have done him serious harm if he had been there at the time. He managed to win the election by a narrow margin, although his victory seems to have inspired some of those who voted against him to consider more violent means. McGee ultimately softened his attitude somewhat, probably for political reasons. Speaking in Montreal on November 14, he declared, "These men deserved death." Many of the members of the audience hissed at him, and it was only after they had fallen silent that he added, "The spirit of our times is opposed to capital punishment."

But that did not seem to be the case when court proceedings began in October. Although many of the prisoners had been released after preliminary hearings in the summer, enough remained in custody for their trials to generate considerable interest. The charges were "having feloniously entered Canada . . . with the intent to levy war against Her

Majesty, and with being found in arms against Her Majesty here." Any Fenians who had been born in Ireland were also charged with treason. On October 24, the trial of "Colonel" Robert B. Lynch began. According to prosecutors, Lynch was in charge of a group of Fenians at Fort Erie, but his defence team argued that he had merely been in Canada as a reporter. The jury remained unconvinced, taking just ninety minutes to find Lynch guilty. He was promptly sentenced to hang on December 13.

The second man to go on trial was John McMahon, a priest from Indiana who was travelling to Montreal to deal with his brother's estate when he had been captured by Fenians and forced to serve as their chaplain. Although evidence was given that he administered to soldiers on both sides, the jury returned the same verdict as they had for Lynch. Again, the judge handed down a sentence of death.

Almost from the time the prisoners were taken into custody, both the British and the Americans had carefully watched proceedings. The British, in particular, were anxious to prevent any of the Fenians from going to the gallows, convinced that this would only create martyrs who would inspire further action from the Fenian Brotherhood. To some extent, that sentiment was echoed in the United States, but with an additional concern. While a large number of Fenians were Irishmen, a considerable number were either native-born or naturalized American citizens. Although some Americans thought they deserved any punishment they got, there was also a vocal part of the population who argued that no American should be executed, and that if executions did take place, the U.S. would be justified in invading and taking over Canada.

Complicating matters further were the precarious relations between Britain and the U.S., who were still negotiating settlements for British activities that led to Union losses during the American Civil War. And, if all this was not enough, there was the matter of the U.S. congressional elections, slated for November. The Irish vote was still considered important enough for both Democrats and Republicans to make the treatment of the Fenian prisoners part of their campaigns. As these progressed, their were calls to stop further trials involving Fenian breach of Canadian neutrality. In a bid to gain more Irish votes for his Republican party, President Andrew Johnson ordered the U.S. courts to drop any outstanding charges against Fenians who had invaded Canada. Then, in a move that likely outraged many but was probably most welcome by the Fenians, Johnson ordered that all arms that had been seized from the invaders be returned to them.

When Fenian prisoners in Canada went to court, there was also considerable discussion about whether or not the trials were being conducted fairly. One issue that angered Irish Catholics was the fact that no Catholics served on the Toronto jury. Another point for debate was the absence of John O'Neill and other top officers. They could not enter

Canada without risking arrest, but their testimony might have shifted the blame from the men to the leadership. Under those circumstances, though, O'Neill and his lieutenants likely would have faced trial on their own, with more severe punishment than was ultimately given to the men they had commanded.

After hearing that Lynch and McMahon had been sentenced to death, American Secretary of State William H. Seward contacted the British government, asking them to intervene. Although Canada was on the brink of nationhood — future prime minister John A. Macdonald would sail for a Confederation conference in London, England, midway through the Fenian trials — Britain still had the final say on the prisoners' fate. Macdonald was content to leave it that way, even though the Canadian governor general, Lord Monck, was very concerned about the consequences executions might bring.

The decision to allow the men to live was made behind the scenes prior to December 13, the date set for the execution of seven of the first men tried. But they were not initially informed of their reprieve. Instead, they were left with the impression that they had received a three-month stay of execution.

By this time, the Fenians captured in Quebec were facing trial in Sweetsburg, Canada East (near Cowansville, southeast of Montreal). Proceedings took up most of the month of December, and by the end only three of the sixteen men originally captured had been sentenced to hang. The small proportion destined for the gallows caused outrage and demands of an investigation, but before that could happen, all ten received commuted sentences. On January 3, it was learned that they would each serve twenty years of hard labour in Kingston Penitentiary.

In spite of these manoeuvres, when the Toronto trials resumed after the Christmas recess, another fifteen men were convicted and sentenced to death. The decision to impose capital punishment was almost certainly a tactic to send a clear message to the Irish Republican Brotherhood, as well as to the general public, that their actions were deserving of death, but the Crown had chosen to be merciful. Many were disappointed with the decision, not the least of whom was William Roberts, one of the Fenian leaders, who fully realized the propaganda value an execution would have for the cause.

As it turned out, not one of the Fenians convicted served anything near twenty years in prison. One man, Thomas Maxwell, died in custody in September 1869. By that time, some of his comrades had already been freed, including John O'Connor. He was out by April 4, 1867, just a few weeks after being transported to Kingston. The last of the Fenian prisoners was released in July 1872, having served only a quarter of his sentence.

Chapter 7
Naval Patrols

While the *Robb* was quick to action when the Fenians crossed the Niagara River, the Canadian Ministry of Marine had to scramble to find suitable vessels to defend its inland waters. Canada had no navy, and the large warships of the British fleet could not make the journey through the shallow waters en route to the Great Lakes. Amid fears that the Fenians were creating a flotilla, the government fell back on a practice that had once been common in the Royal Navy, using fishing tugs and commercial vessels for defence.

The first three boats put into service after the *Robb* were the *Royal*, which was based in Montreal and chartered on June 2; the *Hercules*; and *Canada*, chartered on June 3.

These were armed with guns from two British ships, *Pylades* and *Aurora*. Eleven other vessels were also leased from individuals or private companies: *Metamoras, St. Andrew, Rescue, Hercules #2, Magnet, Watertown, Prince Alfred, Lione, Gordon, British America,* and *Satellite*.

The lease for the *Royal* was typical. Owned by James and Denis Gaherty of J & D Gaherty & Co, she was a relatively new 146-ton vessel. The government offered $120 Canadian per day, with the Gahertys required to provide fuel for the first twenty-four hours of service, plus pay the salary of a crew consisting of a captain, engineer, three firemen, three deckhands, and a pilot for the waters between Bic, Quebec, and Kingston, Ontario. Except for the pilot, whose services would only be needed for a short period of time, the total monthly cost of salaries was around $150. The crew would be augmented by sailors and marines from British vessels, who were sent by either boat or rail from Halifax and other eastern ports. Once on duty, they were armed with a rifle, revolver, and cutlass in the case of the sailors, and a rifle and revolver in the case of the marines.

Meanwhile, communities that had naval brigades wanted to get in on the action. This occasionally caused some problems. Captain Algernon De Horsey sent a crew from HMS *Aurora* to man the *Rescue* when it was docked in Toronto, but when they arrived they discovered the volunteer Toronto Naval Brigade had sailed away to patrol the Windsor area with the newly armed gunboat. A very irritated

De Horsey asked the governor general for another vessel. Monck offered the *Magnet*, which De Horsey rejected as unsuitable and too expensive to refit. While all this was going on the men from the *Aurora* caught up with the *Rescue* in Windsor and relieved the Toronto Naval Brigade. The volunteers returned to Toronto where they took over the *Magnet*.

Most of the leased boats were in service for just three weeks, until fears of another invasion subsided. Others stayed on patrol for longer periods, notably *St. Andrew* and *Royal*. The *Rescue* and *Prince Alfred*, which were initially leased, were soon purchased. By November 1, 1867, the Canadian government would spend $126,632 on gunboats, including $70,348 for leases, $37,787.50 for outright purchases, $4279.50 for equipment, $3272 for repairs, and $10,945 for iron-plating seven steamers.

As arrangements were being made for naval defence, Gilbert McMicken's spy network provided information on what American vessels were on the lakes. Although an April government report had included seven, McMicken's listed nine. Most of these were "revenue steamers" and more concerned about smugglers and poachers, but there were fears that the armed vessels might be commandeered by Fenians or authorized by the United States government to attack Canada. From McMicken's point of view, their speed — usually given at sixteen miles per hour — was worrisome, because many of the boats in use by the Canadian government were considerably slower. This was one of the reasons that both

Captain De Horsey and George Wyatt, the agent in charge of leasing and purchasing gunboats for the government, encouraged the government to continue to keep in service the *Rescue*, which could get up to eleven or twelve miles per hour, a good speed at the time. De Horsey also authorized the purchase of the *Michigan* (not to be confused with the U.S. gunboat *Michigan*, which had patrolled the Niagara area at the time of O'Neill's attack), not only to save money but also to provide more suitable craft for patrolling the lakes.

The *Rescue* was a three-decked wooden sloop with a heavy hull coated in three-eighth-inch plate "sufficient to resist bullets." One hundred and twenty-one feet long, twenty-three feet wide and ten feet deep, she had two engines with a combined one hundred horsepower. Fuelled by coal or wood, she was fast and able to travel through all the canals and rivers between Fort William (Thunder Bay) and Quebec City. In addition, she could accommodate between 200 and 250 troops if necessary. By July 5, 1866, after about a month in government service, she was fitted with two guns amidship and another gun forward.

The *Michigan*, a "propeller boat," had one screw engine and was capable of transporting up to three hundred troops if required. While her hull was substantial and she was able to travel between thirteen and fourteen miles per hour, she lacked masts, small boats, life preservers, and other equipment necessary to make her suitable for government needs. She also had the disadvantage of drawing too much water to navigate the St. Lawrence and the canals of Ontario and Quebec. Once purchased, the *Michigan* was promptly renamed *Prince Alfred*, both to avoid confusion with the American vessel of the same name and to honour a sailor son of Queen Victoria.

While most Canadians may not have been aware of the details of the government's efforts to assemble a suitable fleet of gunboats, enough information was available to prompt rumours that Canada was forming her own navy, or, at the very least, enlisting sailors to man the government gunboats. Predictably, a number of individuals sought employment. Sometimes their applications included recommendations from politicians. Captain Alexander McDonald wrote from the Windsor area on July 21 asking to be hired as master of the *Michigan*. On July 27 two MPPs, Walter McCrea and Archibald Allan, recommended Robert McCorquodale of Chatham as a pilot for one of the gunboats on the upper lakes. Accompanying the letter was a testimonial to McCorquodale's experience and trustworthiness, signed by twenty-three individuals. William McDougall of the ministry of marine replied diplomatically, saying that if a pilot was required he would be happy to consider McCorquodale. With two elected representatives supporting McCorquodale, McDougall had had to tread carefully; but he was not always so diplomatic. When Captain Alexander Cameron asked to be appointed master of the *Prince Alfred* McDougall replied tersely, "I have no knowledge of there being a vacancy in the command of that steamer."

The applicants may not have been so eager to work on the gunboats had they been aware of some of the problems faced by those who were hired. On October 6, as the end of the navigation season neared, James Rice, first engineer on *Prince Alfred*, complained that the $25 monthly salary paid to the second engineer was too low, the incumbent was leaving, and he could not get anyone with the required knowledge and skill for the salary offered. Rice also complained about his own wages, which were $50 per month. Four days later, Lieutenant J. Maxwell Heron, commander of the *Prince Alfred*, added his views on the matter. In his opinion, both engineers were "first rate men" but the second engineer was leaving unless he received a $10 increase. "I think it will be a great pity to lose so good a man . . . Between them they have improved the working of the engine greatly & put it to rights for it was . . . going to the dogs."

While suitable arrangements were being made for the defence of the Great Lakes by Canadian boats, authorities also turned to the British navy for assistance. On June 19, Lord Monck asked for four gunboats for service on the Great Lakes, the number recommended by a British expert sent from the embassy in Washington, DC, to assess the situation. Three were deployed. The boats chosen for duty in Canadian waters belonged to the *Britomart* class, the only suitable vessels that could navigate the shallow canals joining the St. Lawrence and the Great Lakes. Twenty were planned (and sixteen built) during the 1860s. The *Britomart*, which gave her name to the class, was the first. She had a 105'8" keel, was 22'1" across the beam, displaced 330 tons and was equipped with a two-cylinder reciprocating sixty-horsepower steam engine. A three-masted, bark-rigged boat with a smokestack mounted on hinges just forward of midships, she drew only eight feet of water and could reach a speed of nine knots. She was also armed with two 68-pounder Armstrong guns and could carry a crew of approximately forty officers and men, including marines. She was commanded by Lieutenant Arthur Hildebrand Alington. The other two gunboats were the *Cherub*, commanded by Lieutenant Spencer Robert Huntley, and *Heron*, commanded by Lieutenant Henry Frederick Stephenson. It was the first command for both Alington and Stephenson.

The three gunboats had sailed up the eastern coast of North America to Halifax. Until that point few arms were aboard, for fear that a foray into American waters might violate neutrality laws. In Halifax the arms were loaded, and the boats steamed up the St. Lawrence, past Montreal and through the Lachine Canal, where the *Britomart* suffered some damage to her propeller. Although she could rely on her sails for power, to avoid delays both the *Cherub* and *Heron* towed her for parts of the journey. Repairs were eventually made in Port Dalhousie (St. Catharines).

The progress of the gunboats was reported in newspapers in Quebec and Ontario and watched with considerable excitement by the public. The gunboats were a

Her Majesty's gunboat Britomart

tangible reminder of British naval strength, evoking memories of "gunboat diplomacy," when the mere presence of
armed British vessels was enough to prevent hostilities from
breaking out. In addition, there were still some who recalled
the War of 1812, when the fate of Upper Canada, and, to some
extent, all of British North America, relied heavily on which
side had the upper hand on the Great Lakes. Plus there was the
legendary image of the British sailor, the stalwart, dedicated
"jolly tar" who was in the forefront of bringing British law
and order to far-flung corners of the globe. After the Fenian

victory at Ridgeway, the people living on the shores of the Great Lakes were highly relieved at the imminent arrival of British boats, which could repel further attacks. And they wanted to demonstrate their appreciation and admiration by meeting the crews of the gunboats face to face.

As a result, the *Britomart, Cherub*, and *Heron* were as much involved in an extensive public relations campaign as much as they were in naval defence. As the gunboats made their way along the St. Lawrence and into the Great Lakes, the residents of various towns turned out in large numbers. The gunboats reached Kingston harbour on the night of August 6-7. The following morning, a large crowd gathered at the docks to welcome them.

Kingston had the equipment and expertise to repair the *Britomart*'s broken propeller, but in order to do so at least one of her guns would need to be removed. Commander Alington would not agree to this, so it was decided to tow her down the lake for repairs. The *Heron* remained in Kingston for a few days. On Thursday, August 9, the boat's officers were invited to dine at the mess of the Royal Canadian Rifles. On the weekend, decorated with flags and bunting, the boat was opened to visitors. Hundreds turned out and were very pleased with what they saw, according to the *Daily News*. "The 'Jolly Tars' were very courteous and obliging, and went a good ways to entertain their visitors, who were generally well pleased with the appearance of the vessel and the discipline and regularity that prevailed on board."

Wherever they went, the gunboats and their crews were greeted with cheers, celebrations, and frequently a dinner in their honour. Typically these dinners were all-male affairs, with considerable drinking, a certain amount of singing, and some speech-making. Usually, the commanding officer of the gunboat responded with some variation on the theme that the sailors were just doing their duty, and were merely representatives of the British navy and the Empire she defended. The result, both at the dinners, and in response to newspaper reports, tended to be an upsurge of patriotism and a enhanced feeling of security. With such men on hand, there was little need to fear a Fenian invasion.

Of course, things were not as perfect as they seemed. There were discipline problems, with a number of sailors from the gunboats sent to local jails for petty crimes, including drunkenness. There were also desertions. Occasionally, complaints about the sailors' behaviour crept into the newspapers, but these were few and far between. Mostly, the crews of the gunboats were praised, even though they never actually encountered the enemy.

The *Heron* was assigned to patrol Lake Ontario and was based in Toronto. The *Britomart* was stationed in Dunnville, although she made regular, almost weekly, trips to Port Dover, a short distance westward. The *Cherub* was sent to Goderich, on Lake Huron. As the end of the 1866 navigation season drew to a close, the British admiralty advised that it would be withdrawing the three boats from the lakes.

Lord Monck was horrified. There was some feeling that the Fenians would attack again in the spring, as soon as it was possible to travel on the lakes. If the gunboats were sent away, they could not get back to the Great Lakes in time to provide much defence. Monck had his way. The three boats were housed in with lumber for the winter so that their crews would be somewhat more comfortable. The vessels stayed, frozen in the ice, in Toronto, Dunnville, and Goderich. The *Rescue* was also left in Dunnville, although her crew was sent east. In event of emergency, trains could carry the crews back to the boats.

The boats remained on the lakes until late 1868. During that time, there were occasional false alarms when unidentified vessels were seen in the district, as well as rumours of impending Fenian invasions. But the closest the three boats came to any serious action was in the spring of 1868, in the aftermath of D'Arcy McGee's assassination.

In the spring of 1868, McGee was preparing to leave politics. Since the invasion of 1866 and his outspoken comments about how Fenian prisoners should be punished, he had lost significant support in the Irish community. Although he managed to hold on in the 1867 federal election, he had made up his mind to give up his political career. Prime Minister John A. Macdonald had promised him a job in the civil service, and that, plus his interest in literature and history, would be enough to keep him engaged and productive.

After a busy day at the House of Commons, McGee was

making his way home shortly after 2 a.m. on Tuesday, April 7. He lit a cigar and headed for his boarding house, accompanied part of the way by another member of Parliament, Robert MacFarlane. The two parted company as McGee turned on to Sparks Street and walked the final hundred yards to Mrs. Trotters's establishment.

His landlady was still awake, waiting for her son to return home. She later reported hearing footsteps outside the dining room window, then something that sounded like someone at the hall door. As she opened the door, there was a sharp report, resembling that of a firecracker. Outside she saw a figure leaning against the right side of the entranceway. Unsure whom she was looking at, she went for a lamp. By its light she made out blood on her doorway and the figure of a man collapsed on the ground. His face had been blown away by a gunshot.

Six days short of his forty-third birthday, Thomas D'Arcy McGee, rebel, reformer, politician, poet, was dead at the hand of an assassin.

Within twenty-four hours, the police arrested a young tailor, Patrick James Whelan, who had recently moved to Ottawa from Montreal. In his possession were documents that linked him to Fenian organizations, as well as a pistol that had been recently fired. Convinced McGee's murder was politically motivated, the police took Whelan into custody. At his trial, his defence attorney, John Hillyard Cameron — who, ironically, was an Orangeman — discredited some of the witnesses who claimed to have proof that Whelan had stalked McGee with the intent of killing him. Much of the evidence presented was circumstantial and inconclusive, but an all-Protestant jury found Whelan guilty nonetheless. Although there was no proof that he was a Fenian, this was how he was portrayed in the media, and, given McGee's outspoken opposition to Irish Republicanism, many accepted that assessment at face value. Whelan went to the gallows insisting that he was not the assassin, and technically that may have been true. He may not have pulled the trigger, but he claimed to know who did. McGee's biographer, David A. Wilson, believes that, at the very least, Whelan was involved in a plot to murder McGee.

Following the assassination, the gunboats were moved around more than they had been previously. The *Heron* was sent east to patrol the St. Lawrence near Prescott; the *Cherub* was sent from Lake Huron to Lake Ontario, where she was joined the *Britomart* and the *Rescue*. Meanwhile, the *Prince Alfred* was posted to the Detroit River. By July, the *Cherub* was back on the St. Clair River, where she ran aground on Herson's Island. Although the *Prince Alfred* was nearby, worries about a Fenian attack were so profound that, while attempts were made to lighten her and float her off the island, her guns were charged and manned and other precautions taken. A month later both the *Cherub* and the *Britomart* were in the Windsor area, leading the *Detroit Post* to comment that something was "in the wind."

On June 10 the *Kingston Daily Leader* reported, "The several gunboats in the Canadian waters have been placed on a complete war footing. Each one has its full complement of men, and all are well armed and ready."

No further threat materialized, but the very presence of the gunboats seemed to have been an effective deterrent.

That was the argument Monck used with British admiralty, who reasoned that, because there had been no significant attacks, the gunboats were not needed. There was considerable political pressure in Britain to withdraw ships from Canada, especially after Confederation in 1867. Monck objected strenuously. "I consider the maintenance of gunboats on the lakes and river St. Lawrence, the most inexpensive and effective measure that could be adopted for preventing any further attack, or for repelling it, should the invasion be attempted," he wrote to the Duke of Buckingham, secretary of state for the colonies.

As late as October 1868, it seemed the gunboats would remain in Canada for another season. The *Britomart* had already purchased the lumber needed to close herself up for the winter. Then the orders came — the gunboats were to be withdrawn. They had not fired a single shot in anger, but their presence had reassured the populace of Ontario and quite likely minimized the possibility of another Fenian invasion.

Chapter 8
Eccles Hill and Beyond

When the Fenians attacked Quebec in June 1866, a number of them arrived at the home of Asa Westover, a prosperous farmer, and demanded to be fed. Mrs. Westover provided them with a hot meal, which should have been enough had they been following General O'Neill's policy of considerate treatment for civilians. But O'Neill was far away, and the men the Westovers fed repaid their hosts by ransacking the house and stealing valuables. Westover would not forget. In June 1868, at the age of fifty-one, he founded the Missisquoi Home Guard. One of the main purposes of the organization was to defend the area against Fenians and other bandits.

Known as the Red Sashes for the red scarves they wore across their chests, the Home Guard consisted of about thirty men at first. While some of the locals ridiculed them, convinced the Fenian threat was at an end, others weren't so sure. By 1870, membership in the Red Sashes had swelled to more than sixty.

Westover and his lieutenant, Andrew Ten Eyck, made sure the men were well prepared for the possibility of invasion. They were armed with American-manufactured Ballard sporting rifles, which had a reputation for accuracy. Unlike the Enfields that much of the militia had used at Ridgeway, these were breech-loaders, which meant they could be fired faster. The Home Guard also drilled regularly and laid out a careful strategy that would be implemented in case of another invasion.

In 1870, their diligence paid off. The four years following Ridgeway had not been easy ones for the Fenians. Although O'Neill had won the battle at Ridgeway and the skirmish as Fort Erie, the Fenians had been unable to consolidate these victories into a permanent occupation of Canada and place pressure on the British to free Ireland. The organization was also plagued by inner turmoil, so much so that not everyone supported another foray into Canada. O'Neill, however, was willing to try again, firmly believing he could muster as many as six thousand men.

A two-pronged attack was planned. One part, launched from St. Albans, Vermont, would focus on Eccles Hill.

The second, out of Malone, New York, would centre on Holbrook's Corners. The railway did not reach either place, so the Fenians were confident they would have time to seize Canadian territory before any significant number of defenders arrived. In addition, both places were close to the border, so when the British-Canadian troops did materialize, it would be fairly easy to withdraw to safety. Victory, in this case, did not matter so much as the propaganda value of seizing and holding Canadian territory for at least a few hours.

The date chosen for the 1870 invasion was May 24, Queen Victoria's birthday. On May 23, Fenians began to gather in Franklin, Vermont, just across the border from Missisquoi County. They camped at a farmhouse just outside town, waiting for O'Neill to give the orders to proceed.

Canadian and American authorities were well aware of what was going on, but realized the Fenians could not be charged for simply gathering armaments near the border. They were prepared to watch and wait, but U.S. president Ulysses S. Grant was far less patient with the Fenians than his predecessor had been. On May 24, he issued a proclamation against them and ordered soldiers to go to Rouses Point, New York, close to the Canadian border.

O'Neill, meanwhile, had decided to wait an extra day, in hopes that more men would join his forces. Once the proclamation was issued, U.S. Marshall George P. Foster accosted O'Neill and told him to halt his plans for invasion. Foster unfortunately had insufficient backup and O'Neill simply ignored him.

While all this was taking place, the Red Sashes were conducting their own intelligence operation. Among the members of the Home Guard was a fellow by the name of S. N. Hunter, who had previously lived in Vermont. After moving to Canada, he had kept in touch with his former neighbours. On May 23, while visiting Franklin, he learned that the Fenians were poised for an attack. He hurried back to Canada to tell the Home Guard, then returned that evening with a comrade-in-arms to assess the situation. One of the things that caught his attention was the arrival of the first wagonload of Fenian armaments.

Hunter duly reported his findings when he returned to Canada, and the leadership of the Red Sashes alerted the local authorities. They, in turn, sent word to the provincial government, as well as to the assistant commander of the Montreal Military District and to the commander of the local militia. While the Home Guard waited for a response, they put into action the plan that had evolved over the past couple of years. Working on the assumption that the Fenians would target Eccles Hill, they hid behind trees and boulders in the vicinity and waited for the invaders to arrive.

As the hours passed, the men grew impatient. Once more, Hunter headed back to Franklin, Vermont. When he returned, he reported that more than seventy wagons of Fenian weapons, ammunition, and supplies had arrived. Clearly an invasion of considerable size was in the works. Yet the military authorities who had been contacted replied that they did not believe the reports. There had been plenty of false alarms in the past, and neither the assistant commander of the military district nor the commander of the militia seemed prepared to offer any help, and telegraphed messages to that effect.

As it turned out, the seeming lack of interest was a ploy to throw any Fenian informers off track. Information gathered from various sources, including Henri Le Caron, had made it clear to Canadian authorities what was afoot. Around 9 p.m., another telegram arrived from Lieutenant-Colonel Brown Chamberlin of the militia. He was preparing to lead his men to Stanbridge and advised the Home Guard to "pester" any invaders.

Meanwhile, the Home Guard continued to keep an eye on what was happening. Around 3 a.m. on May 25, some of them spotted a heavy wagon making its way along the road near Eccles Hill. When the driver was accosted, he gave a Fenian password. He and his passenger were immediately taken into custody.

By ten that morning, the Home Guard was reinforced by militia from Dunham and Stanbridge. With the thirty-seven Home Guard, this brought the strength of the defenders to eighty men.

They probably were not aware of exactly how many Fenians were waiting to cross the border, but the number seems to have been somewhere between six hundred and eight hundred. This meant that the Canadians were greatly outnumbered, especially since some were temporarily off duty. After waiting more than twenty-four hours for the Fenians, Asa Westover decided his men needed a break. He sent half of them to get themselves some breakfast, reducing the number waiting for the invasion to approximately sixty.

O'Neill had waited the extra day in hopes that more men would arrive. By the morning of May 25, he decided it was time to make his move. The order was given at 11 a.m. O'Neill crossed into Canada with about two hundred men, leaving the remainder behind for the time being. They march four abreast across a bridge spanning a small stream at the base of Eccles Hill. The moment they completed the border crossing, the Home Guard started firing. The Fenian flag bearer, John Rowe, was killed instantly. Another Fenian died soon afterwards, while four more were wounded.

Most of the men who had fought at Ridgeway, and probably most of those who invaded Quebec in 1866, had been newly released soldiers, who, by 1870, had found jobs and gone back to a normal civilian life. Partly as a result of this, O'Neill's army included a number of new recruits who had never been in battle. When they realized they were being shot at, the Fenians ran for cover.

Lieutenant-Colonel Osborne Smith, commander of the Montreal militia, was on his way to Stanbridge when the first shots rang out. A Crimean War veteran, he was no stranger to war, and when a messenger arrived apprising him of the engagement at Eccles Hill, he wheeled his horse about and took command of the defenders.

The fighting raged intermittently for three hours, with the Canadians holding a distinct advantage. At one point, Fenian General J. J. Donnelly and about fifty men were in a valley below Eccles Hill. They could return fire, but they could not leave the valley safely, either to attack the Canadians or to withdraw to the American side of the border, even though a second Fenian force was on the Canadians' right, trying to distract them. This group hailed from New York and had arrived some time after the original advance. They were equipped with field cannon, which they used without much effect. The Canadians continued to fire at them and at Donnelly's force.

Unable to stand the tension any longer, Donnelly allowed his men to break and run for a safer location. As they did so, they were shot at by the Canadians, and Donnelly himself was seriously wounded.

Elsewhere, following orders from Osborne Smith, members of the Home Guard and the Sixtieth Missisquoi Battalion charged down the hill towards the New York Fenians, scaring them off and capturing their cannon. The Home Guard kept it as a trophy and later placed it permanently on Eccles Hill. By 6 p.m., the Fenians were moving back into the United States. By this time, O'Neill was under arrest. Earlier that day, he had withdrawn to a farmhouse on the American side of the border and issued orders from there. But he was not able

Canadian defenders at Missisquoi — May 25, 1870

to stay very long, as the owner of the house insisted he leave. This was the opportunity United States Marshal George P. Foster had been waiting for. He took O'Neill into custody at gunpoint for violating neutrality laws.

Watching these proceedings was Henri Le Caron, who was armed and might have interfered but chose not to. The following day, General Spears — the same man who had led the Fenians in the 1866 raid on Quebec — demanded that Le Caron assemble additional guns and ammunition so that they could invade Canada again. Le Caron insisted this would be impossible at such short notice.

114

Spears made do with what armaments he had on hand; Le Caron was not part of his attack. Instead, claiming he was going to visit O'Neill, who at that time was in Burlington, Vermont, Le Caron headed to Rouses Point, New York, then on to Montreal, where he reported his most recent activities to Judge Charles Coursel, one of McMicken's colleagues. Then he continued on to Ottawa, but along the way was identified as a Fenian and arrested. It was only through some persuasive talking that he was able to convince his captors that they should let him continue his journey to the nation's capital. Once there, he was praised for his work — in secret — then sent back to continue his career as a spy.

Spears meanwhile made a half-hearted effort to attack Canada again, this time targeting Holbrook's Corners, Quebec, across the border from Malone, New York. The invasion was led by General George Owen Starr, the same man who had headed the advance force across the Niagara River prior to the Battle of Ridgeway. On May 26, his force of between two hundred and three hundred men crossed into Canada, not quite a kilometre south of Holbrook's Corners. They were quickly repelled by the Fiftieth Huntingdon Borderers, who suffered only one casualty when John Moore received a slight flesh wound on the forehead. The Fenians had one man killed, one wounded, and one taken prisoner. They spent approximately an hour and a half in Canada, only thirty minutes of which involved fighting.

The next day, General George Meade of the U.S. Army

arrived in Malone. About thirteen hundred Fenians had been drawn there by the hope of another invasion, but dispersed when the American troops arrived and arrests for violation of neutrality laws began. A number of Fenians involved in the Quebec raids did go to trial. Many, including John O'Neill, were sentenced to two years in prison. But history repeated itself in October when President Grant pardoned O'Neill and the other Fenians and set them free.

Almost immediately, O'Neill became involved in another plot to attack Canada. Most Fenians were no longer interested in military action, which they felt was too expensive and generally ineffective. But O'Neill was willing to try again when approached by Bernard O'Donoghue, a Fenian and former mathematics teacher who had been treasurer in Louis Riel's provisional government following the Red River Rebellion of 1869–70. Although Manitoba had become a province, there was still quite a bit of dissension among the Métis, enough for O'Donoghue to believe he could count on them for support. His ambition was to set up a provisional government of his own and eventually annex the territory to the United States.

The Fenians and the Métis had much in common. Both were predominantly Roman Catholic, and both felt they had not been well treated by their governments. The situation was enough to make authorities very worried, so much so that at the end of September 1871 Prime Minister John A. Macdonald sent Gilbert McMicken to Manitoba to gather whatever information he could about support for the Fenians in the province.

McMicken found the Métis resentful about unfulfilled government promises and believed there was sufficient cause for alarm. As a result, at McMicken's insistence, on October 3 Lieutenant Governor Adams Archibald asked for volunteers to protect Manitoba against a possible Fenian invasion. The response was enthusiastic, both among the English-speaking residents and the Métis. Louis Riel, who had been approached by O'Donoghue about a Fenian invasion, helped raise a company of defenders and also alerted the lieutenant governor to the plans.

Riel was well aware that O'Donoghue was only interested in the Métis cause if it suited his plans. There were, however, some Métis who believed the Fenians would help them, and on October 5 they were among the invaders who launched an attack on southern Manitoba.

In the days leading up to the invasion, rumours had been circulating that the Fenians had an army of fifteen hundred. In fact, the number was considerably less, between forty and eighty according to Captain Lloyd Wheaton of the U.S. Army.

O'Donoghue led the force on horseback. The group first captured the customs house at the border, then targeted a Hudson's Bay Company trading post in Pembina. Amid rumours that a sizeable force was ready to attack, the post had been deserted. The Fenians also took about twenty prisoners, but their triumph was short-lived. Captain Wheaton led a group of twenty-three soldiers against the invaders, capturing O'Neill and twelve others, along with ninety-four muskets, eleven sabres, and twelve thousand musket cartridges. O'Donoghue escaped temporarily, but was soon captured by Métis.

Before news that the Fenian invasion had been stopped reached Winnipeg, a contingent of two hundred left Fort Garry heading for the border. They got as far as St. Norbert before they heard that their services were no longer needed. There was still considerable worry that another attack might take place, and authorities remained wary for some time. As it turned out, the aborted raid on Pembina was the last Fenian incursion into Canada.

No charges were laid against O'Donoghue, although he was banned from entering Manitoba for several years. O'Neill, on the other hand, again found himself in court. This time, the charges were dropped by an American judge who ruled that invading Canada was not illegal in the United States. O'Neill moved to Nebraska, where he went to work for some land speculators and died of a stroke on January 7, 1877. He was 42.

Three Métis, Isadore Villeneuve, André Jerome St. Matte, and Louison Letendre, were also arrested. The three were actually American citizens, but that did not stop Canadian authorities from laying charges against them. Villeneuve was acquitted and Letendre was convicted, but the jury was unable to reach a verdict in St. Matte's case. While he waited for a second trial in the spring of 1872, he spent time at hard labour at the stone fort in Lower Fort Garry. He was acquitted at the second trial. Meanwhile, Letendre had been sentenced to hang, but, in a repeat of the Fenian trials of 1866, his sentence was commuted to twenty years in prison. He remained in custody until January 1873, when he was told to leave the country until his twenty-year sentence had expired.

Epilogue

The Fenians failed in their plan to capture Canada and use it as a bargaining chip with Great Britain to negotiate independence for Ireland. Instead, the raids helped create a sense of patriotism and national unity. In Canada, one of the most significant results was increased support for Confederation, notably in New Brunswick. The Fenian invasions made it clear that individual provinces could be easy targets for invaders from the south and that there was greater strength in a Confederation.

The political climate in which these events took place in the United States was favourable to territorial expansion, and remained that way for decades. The American government and powerful U.S. politicians often spoke and acted as if "manifest destiny" was certain to involve absorption of Canada one way or another. Some Canadian historians have suggested that it was only the continued colonial connection of Canada to Great Britain, and the unrivalled power of the British Navy with its east and west coast forward bases in Halifax and Victoria, that tempered any American thought of annexation of Canadian territory when circumstances were favourable. Indeed, there was a string of events from 1867 to 1914 when Washington tested Britain's continued commitment to the existence of Canada with its borders now extending all the way to the Pacific. In the light of all this, it's easy to see how the Fenians could have become the advance guard for a real challenge to Canadian territorial integrity from the U.S. had they had more military success. But the combination of British troops, Canadian militia, some inept Fenian leadership, and a good deal of luck forestalled that eventuality.

Official commemoration of the invasions was generally slow in coming, with one exception. On July 1, 1870, just four years after Ridgeway, the Canadian Volunteer Monument was dedicated on the University of Toronto campus, close to Queen's Park. It commemorated the nine men from the Queen's Own Rifles who died at Ridgeway or shortly afterwards and was inscribed with the date of the battle and the words: "Honour the brave who died for their country."

While veterans of the battle, especially those in Ontario, did what they could to keep memories of the invasion alive, it took more than thirty years for any government to provide official recognition. In 1895, the Veterans of '66 association created a petition asking for some kind of official acknowledgement. This finally arrived in January 1899, when Britain organized the Canadian General Service Medal, which was to be distributed to veterans of the 1866 and 1870 raids, as well as to those who had served in the Red River Rebellion. To some extent, the creation of the medal may have been motivated by the need to fan patriotic sentiment in Canada, as Britain was on the brink of the Second Boer War and in the event Canadians did serve in South Africa.

In 1916, on the fiftieth anniversary of the Battle of Ridgeway, a cornerstone was laid at the site of the battle, on what is now Highway 3, north of the town of Ridgeway and about five kilometres west of Fort Erie. A cairn was constructed there and in 1921 the site was designated a National Historic Battlefield. A Province of Ontario historical plaque is also located in the community of Ridgeway, on the east side of Ridge Road North, two-and-a-half blocks south of Dominion Road.

At Eccles Hill, the cannon captured from the Fenians in 1870 forms part of a granite monument that dates back to 1902. The site was officially designated a National Historic Site of Canada in 1923. There is also a marble marker on Eccles Hill indicating the place where elderly Margaret Vincent was accidentally shot by the Royal Welsh Fusiliers.

While Canadians were slowly building monuments connected to the Fenian invasions, the Irish were continuing to fight for independence from Britain. On December 6, 1921, the Anglo-Irish Treaty was signed, which provided for the establishment of the Irish Free State. Two years earlier, President Éamon De Valera had visited the United States in hopes of drumming up support for the Irish cause. While there, he went to Omaha, Nebraska, and on October 28 attended a ceremony dedicating a plaque in honour of John O'Neill, "The Hero of Ridgeway." More recently, in March 2012, a plaque was unveiled near the American side of the Niagara River, marking the spot in Buffalo where the Fenians launched their 1866 raid against Canada.

Epilogue

Today relatively few Canadians are familiar with the Fenians or the impact they had on our history in the years immediately before and after Confederation. That may change, however, as the 150th anniversary of the 1866 invasion approaches and re-enactors and historic groups plan events to remind the public of the invasions that helped shape Canada.

Acknowledgements

The author gratefully acknowledges the following sources that provided quote material in this book: *Turning Back the Fenians: New Brunswick's Last Colonial Campaign*, by Robert L. Dallison; *Dunnville Heroes: The* W.T. Robb *and the Dunnville Naval Brigade in the 1866 Fenian Invasion*, by John Thornley Docker; *The Last Invasion of Canada: The Fenian Raids, 1866–1870*, by Hereward Senior; *Ridgeway: The American Fenian Invasion and the 1866 Battle that Made Canada*, by Peter Vronsky; and *Thomas D'Arcy McGee*, by David A.Wilson.

Material on the gunboats came from numerous sources, including dozens of newspapers and the log books of *Britomart*, *Heron*, and *Cherub*, now in the British National Archives, Kew.

I am particularly indebted to the Dunnville District Heritage Association for its ongoing encouragement and support, and to the Provincial Archives of New Brunswick and Missisquoi Historical Society's Musée Missisquoi Museum for the use of illustrations from their collections.

Finally, I wish to express heartfelt thanks to my publisher, Jim Lorimer, who made some very useful suggestions during early discussions about the book, and especially to my editor, Laurie Miller, whose extensive knowledge and keen sensitivity make working with him a joy. This dynamic duo has made the book much better than it otherwise would have been.

Further Reading

Dallison, Robert L. *Turning Back the Fenians: New Brunswick's Last Colonial Campaign.* Fredericton: Goose Lane Editions and New Brunswick Military Heritage Project, 2006.

Docker, John Thornley. *Dunnville Heroes: The* W. T. Robb *and the Dunnville Naval Brigade in the 1866 Fenian Invasion.* Dunnville: Dunnville District Heritage Association, 2003.

MacDonald, Cheryl. "Henri Le Caron," in *Great Canadian Imposters.* Toronto: James Lorimer & Company Ltd., Publishers, 2009.

Senior, Hereward. *The Last Invasion of Canada: The Fenian Raids, 1866–1870.* Ottawa: Canadian War Museum Historical Publications, 2012.

Vronsky, Peter. *Ridgeway: The American Fenian Invasion and the 1866 Battle that Made Canada.* Toronto: Allen Lane Canada, 2011.

Wilson, David A. *Thomas D'Arcy McGee,* Volumes 1 and 2. Montreal and Kingston: McGill-Queens University Press, 2008 and 2011.

About the Author

Cheryl MacDonald has written extensively about Canadian history over the last thirty-five years. For more than twenty-five years she was author of a weekly heritage column in the Simcoe *Times-Reformer*. She has also written more than forty books, including such Amazing Stories titles as *Isaac Brock*, *Lethal Ladies*, and *Shipwrecks of the Great Lakes*. In 2012 she was awarded a Queen Elizabeth Diamond Jubilee Medal in recognition of "decades steadfastly dedicated to documenting and promoting" local history.

Photo Credits

Chapter 1 — D'Arcy McGee; Library & Archives Canada, 21541

Chapter 2 — Gilbert McMicken; Library & Archives Canada

Chapter 3 — York County Militia; Provincial Archives of New Brunswick, George Taylor fonds: P5-151

Chapter 4 — John O'Neill; Library & Archives Canada, C-050394

Chapter 5 — Battle of Ridgeway; Library & Archives Canada, C-018737

Chapter 6 — First Invasion of Quebec; Library & Archives Canada, C-11731

Chapter 7 — Her Majesty's gunboat *Britomart*; Haldimand County Museum

Chapter 8 — Canadian defenders, May 25, 1870; Musée Missisquoi Museum

Index